IN THE BEST POSSIBLE LIGHT

BENETH PETERS JONES

BJU PRESS

GREENVILLE, SOUTH CAROLINA

Library of Congress Cataloging-in-Publication Data

Jones, Beneth Peters, 1937-
  In the best possible light / Beneth Peters Jones.
    p. cm.
  ISBN 1-59166-259-1 (pbk. : alk. paper)
  1. Christian women—Religious life. 2. Etiquette for women. 3. Beauty,
Personal. I. Title.
  BV4527.J665 2004
  248.8'43—dc22

                                                            2004006349

Cover illustration: PhotoDisc

All Scripture is quoted from the Authorized King James Version unless otherwise noted.

In the Best Possible Light

Cover design by Jamie Miller
Composition by Melissa Matos

©2004 by BJU Press
Greenville, South Carolina 29614

Printed in the United States of America
All rights reserved

ISBN 1-59166-259-1
15 14 13 12 11 10 9 8 7 6 5 4 3 2 1

For Emily and Kate—beloved granddaughters.
May they grow to be ladies of the Light.

Table of Contents

Acknowledgments

A book becomes reality only through the efforts of many people. I'm deeply grateful to each one, named and unnamed, who had a part in creating *In the Best Possible Light*. My editor, Suzette Jordan, is a joy to work with. Her positive spirit buoyed my own more times than she could know. Kudos, too, to those technological folks who often rescued me from hair-tearing frustration with my computer's noncooperation. Special thanks are due the dear Hamilton family in Fairbanks, Alaska, who graciously provided a full week of writing opportunity at the most critical pre-deadline point. And, finally, abundant thanks to Jennifer Sackett, without whose hours of research this new edition could never have been completed.

Foreword

Once a completed manuscript takes its trip to the BJU Press, it's like a child grown and flown. The printed product creates a warm sense of fulfillment, but I never go back and read it. So when I received the working text of *Beauty and the Best* from the Press with their request to update and revise it, I was jolted to realize how much of life's vapor lies between the original writing and this rewrite. Among other things, the original was laboriously composed and corrected on typewriters—this revision on work-easing computers. The first was written while our children were still at home; this second when they're grown, involved in various ministries, and rearing families of their own. The early 1980s were different times, and Christian women were closer to Scripture and freer from cultural dictates. Therefore, the following pages really are much more total rewrite than mere revision.

Just as times have changed in the past twenty years, so have people. The general spiritual degeneration so evident throughout our culture can come as no surprise except for the speed with which it has happened: the Bible has clearly foretold it. The heartbreaking surprise, however, is that Christians have not just accommodated the deterioration—they have adopted it into their own lifestyles. In the 1980s a rather generalized approach to the topic of Christian womanhood seemed sufficient: it could be taken for granted that Christian girls and women were personally spending time in the Word of God and were looking to it for their standards. That assumption can no longer be made. My constant contacts with women young and old across America make it unavoidably evident that the Bible has become the *last* thing they would consult for direction in daily living. I weep over the sad harvest in lives where the world's weeds have been allowed to flourish.

Besides weeping, though, I've been moved to make considerable adjustment in this presentation. More practical specifics are given, and a great deal more Scripture.

As with the original, so too with this: it comes in response to the urging of friends and from my own increasing heart burden for girls and women in their struggle to establish and maintain godly femininity in an ungodly age. America's worsening paganism demands that we believers preserve, defend, demonstrate, and illustrate the "*faith once delivered to the saints.*" This rewritten text is addressed specifically to those last two points: demonstration and illustration that there *is* light: light that gives life, warmth, and beauty to womanhood. It is the Light of life—the Lord Jesus Christ.

Prayerfully in His love and mine,

CHAPTER ONE

The Beauty of Light

CHAPTER ONE

The Beauty of Light

For God, who commanded the light to shine out of darkness, hath shined in our hearts, to give the light of the knowledge of the glory of God in the face of Jesus Christ. **II Cor. 4:6**

Standard "how-to" books on feminine beauty can range from painfully silly to revoltingly crude. Their philosophy and their purpose are skewed. That's inevitable because they overlook or deny the most important aspect of the human self and its existence: the spiritual. So, then, the beauty they tout really is only skin deep. What a waste, and what a shame.

The world's beauty emphasis is only to be expected, and it shouldn't surprise us. But it is sad to see that, rather than recognizing and rejecting the secular approach to womanly beauty, many Christians accept and adopt it. Why? How is it that saved girls and women can so readily fall prey to worldly blandishments? I believe that primarily the weakness lies in compartmentalizing life. That is, "spiritual" is the church; everything else is secular.

For those of us who are born again, the spiritual dimension isn't to be an isolated compartment; it should be the vital core of self and life. We're told in Genesis that when God created the first human being, *"man became a living soul."* We occupy this body of flesh only a brief time, but our soul lives forever. According to the infallible, forever-settled Word of God, a

3

person's soul continues to exist either rejoicing in heaven with God or suffering in hell, condemned by God. The determining factor in our eternal destiny is our soul's garb. Every individual chooses his spiritual garments: either gleaming robes of righteousness purchased by the blood of Christ the Savior or the besmirched rags of sin produced by self-effort.

Our temporal being and our eternal one are not meant to be separated from one another, existing in different compartments. The two communicate and interact constantly. Our *"living soul"* is the very essence of our being. Scripture urges us as believers to live in such a way that we reflect not just the unspeakably marvelous work that has been done in our soul but also the mighty Worker, the Lord Jesus Christ.

For whom is this book written? Women everywhere who possess *genuine* internal beauty—beauty that has its source in light. Such beauty is possible only through sin's cleansing by the shed blood of Jesus Christ and the continuing "housework" of the indwelling Holy Spirit.

Our world is full of religious labels. But labels don't count for a thing. God's holy Word, the Bible, makes clear that human beings are helpless to cleanse their own hearts, to purify their own lives, and to make themselves acceptable in the sight of an eternal, holy God.

But we are all as an unclean thing, and all our righteousnesses are as filthy rags; and we all do fade as a leaf; and our iniquities, like the wind, have taken us away. **Isa. 64:6**

Wash you, make you clean; put away the evil of your doings from before mine eyes; cease to do evil. **Isa. 1:16**

Come now, and let us reason together, saith the Lord: though your sins be as scarlet, they shall be as white as snow; though they be red like crimson, they shall be as wool. **Isa. 1:18**

Perhaps you don't like to acknowledge your dark sinfulness; the Bible silences any objections by saying,

for all have sinned, and come short of the glory of God. **Rom. 3:23**

Rather than deny our sinfulness, God calls upon us to *acknowledge* the filth of our sins and to bring them to Him for cleansing:

If we confess our sins, he is faithful and just to forgive us our sins, and to cleanse us from all unrighteousness. **I John 1:9**

Why ask God to remove our sins? Because otherwise a righteous and just God must condemn our sin and punish it. He proclaimed long ago through Ezekiel,

the soul that sinneth, it shall die. **Ezek. 18:20**

The truth was reiterated by the apostle Paul, with the cure for sin added:

For the wages of sin is death; but the gift of God is eternal life through Jesus Christ our Lord. **Rom. 6:23**

When we acknowledge and confess our sins, God cancels our punishment because Jesus Christ took our sinfulness upon Himself and died on our behalf on the cross of Calvary.

Christ hath redeemed us from the curse of the law, being made a curse for us: for it is written, Cursed is every one that hangeth on a tree. **Gal. 3:13**

Blotting out the handwriting of ordinances that was against us, which was contrary to us, and took it out of the way, nailing it to his cross. **Col. 2:14**

As He cancels our sin debt, He simultaneously extends an eternal gift:

For by grace are ye saved through faith; and that not of yourselves: it is the gift of God: not of works, lest any man should boast. **Eph. 2:8–9**

He that believeth on the Son of God hath the witness in himself: he that believeth not God hath made him a liar; because he believeth not the record that God gave of his Son. And this is the record, that God hath given us eternal life, and this life is in his Son. He that hath the Son hath life; and he that hath not the Son of God hath not life. **I John 5:10–12**

That if thou shalt confess with thy mouth the Lord Jesus, and shalt believe in thine heart that God hath raised him from the dead, thou shalt be saved. For with the heart man believeth unto righteousness; and with the mouth confession is made unto salvation. . . . For whosoever shall call upon the name of the Lord shall be saved. **Rom. 10:9–10, 13**

Saved! Cleansed! Made new by the power of God through the precious blood of His only begotten Son, the Lord Jesus Christ! Jesus said,

I am come a light into the world, that whosoever believeth on me should not abide in darkness. **John 12:46**

Thus, we are brought out of death's darkness into the light of life.

He brought me up also out of an horrible pit, out of the miry clay, and set my feet upon a rock, and established my goings. And he hath put a new song in my mouth, even praise unto our God: many shall see it, and fear, and shall trust in the Lord. **Ps. 40:2–3**

Therefore being justified by faith, we have peace with God through our Lord Jesus Christ. **Rom. 5:1**

We emerge from spiritual darkness and enter into light instantaneously at salvation. It is a gift. But we walk in light *by choice*. The prophet Isaiah long ago challenged,

Come ye, and let us walk in the light of the Lord. **Isa. 2:5b**

Jesus said in John 8:12,

I am the light of the world: he that followeth me shall not walk in darkness, but shall have the light of life.

That chosen path of following Christ more often than not moves in direct opposition to the world's pathway. Only with a heart made clean and lovely by salvation can a woman move toward genuine beauty of self and life.

God's desire is that salvation should begin a process by which we grow spiritually lovelier day by day. The process is called sanctification. Likewise, in matters of our physical self we should engage in thoughtful, consistent effort toward loveliness. Our outward self should be unified with our inner person as we move toward that supreme moment when we'll stand face to face with Him who is "altogether lovely."

There are many ways to approach the subject of a Christian woman's testimony before others. In order to achieve unity and to emphasize pervasive spiritual principles, I've chosen the theme of *light*. In the physical sense, we recognize and opt for the advantage of light over darkness. The very contrast of the terms themselves is something we use often in conversation, description, and instruction.

While an unsaved girl or woman orders her life according to considerations of herself, her feelings, her desires, her ease, and so forth, God's woman must live very differently. The Bible clearly sets forth that principle from Genesis through Revelation: the believer's life focus is to be God Himself. First John 1:5b tells us,

God is light, and in Him is no darkness at all.

Further, the Word declares,

In him we live, and move, and have our being. **Acts 17:28**

Accordingly, we should be *lighted* creatures in every part of our existence.

What, then, is my intended purpose in writing this book? ***To encourage and assist a born-again Christian woman—whether she's twelve or eighty-two—to cultivate her personal feminine loveliness in order to reflect the beauty Jesus Christ has brought to her soul and heart.***

Women in wide-ranging age groups used the original *Beauty and the Best*. This new book is intended to expand on the concepts presented there. Each chapter will first deal with general principles concerning the topic under discussion, followed by **Spiritual X-Rays**, in which we'll encapsulate heart essentials in a Christian's pursuit of beauty. Then a **Generation Considerations** section will address three groups: *teens*, *mothers*, and *mentors*. And finally, chapters will end with **Caution Lights**, giving observations and warnings about imbalance and distortion.

Now let's move ahead together to carefully explore and contemplate various life areas we share as women and in which we have responsibility to seek—and to reflect—the light of the Lord. May the psalmist's prayer become ours.

O send out thy light and thy truth: let them lead me; let them bring me unto thy holy hill, and to thy tabernacles. **Ps. 43:3**

CHAPTER TWO

Femininity's Prism

CHAPTER TWO

Femininity's Prism

Light is sown for the righteous, and gladness for the upright in heart.
Ps. 97:11

The twenty-first century Christian girl or woman exists in a spiritually foreign environment: a world shadowed by sin's darkness, a world
where the bizarre is applauded and the beautiful is ridiculed. Scripture
describes the condition of those among whom we live and from whom we
differ so greatly:

> *Having the understanding darkened, being alienated from the life of God
> through the ignorance that is in them, because of the blindness of their heart:
> who being past feeling have given themselves over unto lasciviousness, to work
> all uncleanness with greediness.* **Eph. 4:18–19**

We should not like or feel comfortable in their dark setting. Yet it's
difficult to buck the secular trends, to swim against the cultural tide.
The difficulties often make us sigh or whine. But why? Human history
has always been rife with conditions just as bad or even worse. Reflect
only briefly on the past, and that fact will be inescapable. With a heavy
heart God has watched and recorded His human creature's earthly passage, with its prevailing evil nurtured by Satan, the god of this world. The
Bible tells us of pre-Noachic wickedness, of the early Middle East's dark
practices and worship. Human history itself records—and tries to explain

or excuse—the wretched excesses of Rome, the spiritual darkness of pre-Reformation Europe, and so forth. On and on it has gone. But the point for us to note is this: in the midst of every dark era there have been some who walked in the light. ***Our historical and cultural setting is no excuse against being and doing right.*** Both secular and religious history reveal the names, stories, and influence of those who have successfully preceded us on the challenging path of light.

Despite surrounding circumstances of deepest darkness, numberless ones walked in spiritual light; a few are familiar to us—Noah, Moses, Joshua, Isaiah, Jeremiah, Daniel. Then came those few who turned the world upside down—the apostles. When darkness again rolled over the earth, others maintained and proclaimed the light—Luther, Zwingli, the Wesleys, missionaries named and nameless . . . indeed ours is a noble heritage! And ours is the challenge for preservation and extension of the light.

"But," you might respond, "I'm no Daniel, no Martin Luther. I'm only a teenager . . . a housewife . . . an office worker . . . a retiree." Whoever and wherever you are, as a child of God you are a bearer of light and have the responsibility to obey Christ's admonition:

> Let your light so shine before men, that they may see your good works, and glorify your Father which is in heaven. **Matt. 5:16**

The effects and influence of spiritual darkness are many; any one of them could be treated at length from the standpoint of the Scripture's light. This study, however, will focus upon one particular area: sin's shadows cast upon womanhood.

One of the greatest—and perhaps least recognized—sources of darkness in Christian women's lives today is the pervasive influence of radical feminism. The tenets of the modern movement are clearly antithetical to Scripture; nevertheless, it is heartbreakingly evident that they have invaded Christian attitudes, actions, and activities. ***The feminist taint in a Christian girl or woman is spiritual garbage that must be removed, and a foundation of Scripture must replace it before we can build a temple of godly femininity.***

While it's impossible to give a thorough history of the feminist movement in America, a thumbnail sketch can help us understand how it has come to its present dark workings.

Unlikely as it may seem, one part of the effective women's movement in our country began with noble aims in the late 1800s, spearheaded by the WCTU—Women's Christian Temperance Union. Frances Willard was the organization's outstanding leader.

Social conditions of the 1800s cried for reform. The nation was awash in liquor. Its production was rampant, and alcoholism—with all its destructive fallout—was a nationwide problem. Men drank away not only their own quality of life but that of their families as well. Women were helpless against the suffering. They were not only barred from voting; they also had no legal rights—they couldn't own property, they had no legal protection against abusive treatment by their husbands, and they couldn't have custody of their children in cases of divorce. In fact, husbands didn't have any legal obligation to support their wives and children.

The aims of the early women's movement were commendable:

- recognition as citizens, with the right to vote
- curtailment of liquor production, sale, and consumption
- protective laws in cases of prostitution and rape
- separate quarters for men and women in prisons

Moreover, in each area of their endeavors, the purpose of "home protection" was strong, and part of each program included Bible studies. Frances Willard made clear statements of the Christian principles she espoused.

Following ratification of the Nineteenth Amendment to the Constitution in 1920, and the (literally) sobering effects of Prohibition, women in general settled to enjoy the fruits of their efforts. Then, as the Second World War pulled women into the production work force to supply materiel, it became clear that there were inequalities in pay scales and advancement opportunities, as well as in access to the professions. Efforts to change the situation were largely random and unorganized.

The modern, organized women's movement began in the 1960s, and its tone was entirely unlike that of the original efforts that had bridged the nineteenth and twentieth centuries. It drew its character from a number of destructive forces unleashed in that critical decade of the sixties:

- Prayer and Bible reading were removed from public schools.
- "God is dead" became the watchword in many colleges and universities.
- Rock-and-roll music promoted sexual revolution.
- The hippies' subculture proclaimed the glories of rootlessness and "free think."

In 1963 Betty Friedan, a spokeswoman for women's rights, published her book *The Feminine Mystique*. It was a steel-toed boot that kicked open the door to radical feminism, and Friedan's followers have marched through the door wearing chain mail and carrying flamethrowers. Their militant proclamations attack a broad Judeo-Christian landscape:

- The church and its teachings are passé.
- We are products of and responsible for "Mother Earth."
- All values are relative; there is no absolute truth.
- There really is no difference between men and women except in the limited sense of biological reproduction (an unalterable fact to despise and discredit).
- Parents should raise their daughters more like boys and their sons more like girls.
- Men are despots.
- Women are victims of male oppression.

Clearly, modern feminists fit God's description:

They are of those that rebel against the light; they know not the ways thereof, nor abide in the paths thereof. **Job 24:13**

The globe of modern feminism turns upon the axis of supreme self-centeredness: every woman has the right to be "fulfilled," or "happy." Any obstacle thwarting that selfish drive is expendable.

With such dark determinations in place, it's not difficult to see how a "fetus" becomes an inconvenience from which a woman has the right to be loosed via abortion. Nor can we respond to that judgment with undue horror. George Barna, the well-known Christian researcher, reports that

39 percent, or one out of three, "born-again Christians" believe it's morally acceptable for couples to live together before marriage!

Among feminists, some seek to reletter their name badge: they'd now like to be called "femaleists." From their viewpoint woman is everything—hence the push to legitimize lesbianism.

As in so many instances, repetition, loudness, whining, and threats have had their effect. Our local newspaper recently set forth an approving definition of today's woman: "strong, savvy, and sexy." Such women are repeatedly, tediously presented on film and in print. They're portrayed as cerebral, tough, immoral, and dirty-mouthed. The touting of that image for roughly fifty years has taken a terrible toll on American society.

The darkness of radical feminism is unmistakable. But what of the shadows it casts into Christian circles? We born-again women—unwittingly, perhaps—are being more influenced by the pervading feminist mindset than by the clearly stated Word of God. Why? The answer is simple, really, when we look at ourselves honestly:

- We neglect spending personal time each day in the Word.
- We limit our spiritual life to within the four walls of our church—roughly four to six hours a week.
- We "live, move, and have our being" in an age that accepts and promotes all the wrong things.
- We constantly ingest spiritual poison via radio, CDs, TV, books, videos, and movies.

Now let's turn to the light of God's Word, praying that it will effectively dispel whatever darkness we may have allowed in our concept and demonstration of femininity. Point by point, the Bible contradicts feminism's dark preaching and practices.

To the law and to the testimony: if they speak not according to this word, it is because there is no light in them. **Isa. 8:20**

This verse immediately identifies modern feminism as a dark entity. But its influence is long-standing, deeply entrenched, and unceasingly reiterated politically, socially, and educationally. Most of us who claim to be Christians are rightly appalled at the brazen, unnatural claims and aims of the movement, yet to a large degree we've bought into its spirit. It behooves us, then, not just to recognize the trash pile but also to replace it with the essential foundation for lighted womanhood.

Let's start at the beginning—where a basic truth enrages feminism's proponents: God created woman.

> *So God created man in his own image, in the image of God created he him: male and female created he them.* **Gen. 1:27**

> *And the Lord God caused a deep sleep to fall upon Adam, and he slept: and he took one of his ribs, and closed up the flesh instead thereof; and the rib, which the Lord God had taken from man, made he a woman, and brought her unto the man. And Adam said, This is now bone of my bones, and flesh of my flesh: she shall be called Woman, because she was taken out of Man.*
> **Gen. 2:21–23**

These passages show us both woman's distinct, marvelous beginning and her created role as an essential complement to man. It should be no surprise that feminists not only are rabid evolutionists but that they also lead in blasphemous claims of a feminine god and the production of a gender-neutral "bible." O that we who embrace the eternal Truth would be more faithful in its defense and proclamation!

All the discussions to follow will seek to bring a Scripture perspective to our practical concerns as women. But in this "clearing out" opening, it's important to counteract feminism's murky essence with basic Bible enlightenment.

The precepts espoused by radical feminism spring from its core motivation: hatred of and revolt against God and His Word. Close your ears to their raucous claims, Christian woman, and open your heart afresh to what God Himself proclaims:

> *I am the Lord, and there is none else, there is no God beside me.* **Isa. 45:5**

> *I have made the earth, and created man upon it: I, even my hands, have stretched out the heavens, and all their host have I commanded.* **Isa. 45:12**

> *I, even I, am the Lord: and beside me there is no saviour.* **Isa. 43:11**

Besides pronouncing His own identity, God makes unequivocal statements concerning His written Word:

> So shall my word be that goeth forth out of my mouth: it shall not return unto me void, but it shall accomplish that which I please, and it shall prosper in the thing whereto I sent it. **Isa. 55:11**

> The grass withereth, the flower fadeth: but the word of our God shall stand for ever. **Isa. 40:8**

> Heaven and earth shall pass away, but my words shall not pass away. **Matt. 24:35**

> For verily I say unto you, Till heaven and earth pass, one jot or one tittle shall in no wise pass from the law, till all be fulfilled. **Matt. 5:18**

Rather than adhering only to a written message, genuine Christianity is a living faith in the Living Word:

> In the beginning was the Word, and the Word was with God, and the Word was God. . . . All things were made by him; and without him was not any thing made that was made. In him was life; and the life was the light of men. . . . And the Word was made flesh, and dwelt among us, (and we beheld his glory, the glory as of the only begotten of the Father,) full of grace and truth. **John 1:1, 3–4, 14**

In a conversation with Simon Peter, Jesus asked the disciple for his belief in Jesus' identity. Peter responded, "Thou art the Christ, the Son of the living God." Jesus then said of His identity as God,

> Upon this rock I will build my church; and the gates of hell shall not prevail against it. **Matt. 16:18**

God's Word makes clear from beginning to end that His interest in and will for us are not limited to our doings; they address our very essence. Part of that essence for you and me, surely, is our divinely created womanhood. So, then, in a general sense and to buttress ourselves against feminism's distortions, what can we find in the Bible about women?

First, there are general outlines indicating God's heart for women. Think back to some of the earliest pages of the Old Testament; consider the written Law, with its attendant statutes. One aspect of God's command against adultery is that it focuses protective care upon women. He builds that protective wall higher and stronger as He forbids rape and incest. The New Testament opens with clear indications that throughout His earthly life Jesus honored women, dealt tenderly with them, and in turn valued their ministry to and for Him. The book of Acts and the Epistles refer to many women who are extolled because of their faith and their lives' value—not only to the apostles but also to the fledgling church as a whole.

Besides the aforementioned sketches that indicate God's attitude toward women, He has given us Old Testament and New Testament snapshots of admirable women, and a three-dimensional, full-color portrait of ideal womanhood in Proverbs 31. No matter how many times you read that familiar chapter, you'll not find a trace of feminism's spirit. We will refer to that grand lady in following chapters as her characteristics apply to our considerations.

And, third, God through the apostle Paul makes it clear that we women are to occupy a place secondary to man. Again, here's a Bible truth that makes steam come from a feminist's ears. But you and I can rightly *delight* in our assignment. What a wonderful place of honor and protection!

> *But I would have you know, that the head of every man is Christ; and the head of the woman is the man; and the head of Christ is God.* **I Cor. 11:3**

> *Nevertheless neither is the man without the woman, neither the woman without the man, in the Lord.* **I Cor. 11:11**

> *Wives, submit yourselves unto your own husbands, as it is fit in the Lord.* **Col. 3:18**

There are evidences all around us that real femininity is rapidly vanishing from the American scene. Feminists have so shouted, belittled, and militated against woman's "slavish" lot that many throughout the land have concluded that femininity—and its refinement—really is archaic.

The vital fact to remember in the midst of all the claims, catcalls, and confusion is that *God has not changed His mind.* As He designed femininity, so He desires femininity.

Go back through the tenets and characteristics of modern feminism listed earlier. It's not difficult to discern that it is *against God Himself* the "women's liberation" efforts are ultimately aimed. Most certainly, then, its purposes and its spirit should be rejected by those who know and love God through His Son Jesus Christ.

But can we be *happy* in the "confines" of femininity? Supremely so! Unsaved definers of "beauty" contribute to secularism's overall efforts to redefine womanhood by destroying traditional and biblical distinctives. That destruction doesn't bring real betterment of any sort. Every precept established by God is given *for our benefit.*

For I know the thoughts that I think toward you, saith the Lord, thoughts of peace, and not of evil, to give you an expected end. **Jer. 29:11**

Over and over again throughout His Word, God tells us that when we obey Him, we will be blessed; when we disobey, we'll experience blight. Yet, just as in the Garden of Eden, we human beings resent, resist, and disobey God's instructions. Our flesh consistently wants its own way—though the self way is a path of shadows. Shadows mark the faces of those who most vehemently deny Truth: hardness, disillusionment, and bitter emptiness result from disregarding the Almighty's verities. God through Solomon might have been describing feminism's self-promoting adherents in Proverbs 9:13—

A foolish woman is clamorous: she is simple, and knoweth nothing.

Blood-bought girls and women who seek to walk in the light of the Lord should consistently and diligently seek to fulfill God's purpose for our being. That demands establishing and maintaining standards that surpass the merely *acceptable.* What, then, should be our specific personal goal? Simply put, it's this: **excellence in every aspect.** Pursuing excellence must never be for the sake of self but always for the sake of our excellent God.

Touching the Almighty, we cannot find him out: he is excellent in power, and in judgment, and in plenty of justice: he will not afflict. **Job 37:23**

O Lord our Lord, how excellent is thy name in all the earth! who hast set thy glory above the heavens. **Ps. 8:1**

Sing unto the Lord; for he hath done excellent things: this is known in all the earth. **Isa. 12:5**

That ye may approve things that are excellent; that ye may be sincere and without offence till the day of Christ; being filled with the fruits of righteousness, which are by Jesus Christ, unto the glory and praise of God. **Phil. 1:10–11**

How dare we be less excellent and do less than excellently for our Creator, Redeemer, and King? To settle for less than the finest femininity is to be a thief several times over:

- We rob God of the fulfillment of His perfect plan.
- We rob other women of an inspirational, gracious touch and example.
- We rob the men around us of the opportunity to exercise the protective, gentlemanly considerations native to their masculinity.
- We rob ourselves of the beauty possible only in conformity to divine will.

So, then, what is this excellence of feminine beauty we're to seek? Is beauty the same as *prettiness*? No. The first definition of beauty given by *The American Heritage Dictionary* (3rd ed., 1992) is "a delightful quality associated with harmony of form or color, excellence of craftsmanship, truthfulness, originality, or another property." That's a much broader definition than is ordinarily operative in our minds. It should be a tremendous encouragement to every one of us. Proverbs 31 reminds us that beauty in and of itself is "vain," or empty and meaningless. But so is virtually *every* attribute and accomplishment of human beings, the writer of Ecclesiastes reminds us, if it is pursued for its own sake. On the other hand, beauty is a worthy goal for every Christian woman if we

- recognize that our soul has been made beautiful by our altogether lovely Lord
- desire discernible beauty as demonstrative of His original design in creating femininity
- seek to be reflectors of His beautiful holiness

These are matters the unsaved world would never consider—but the saved woman or girl must never forget! Proverbs 31:10 notes the rarity and the value of she who knows and walks in the light of the Lord:

Who can find a virtuous woman? for her price is far above rubies.

Spiritual X-Rays

Take heed to yourselves, that your heart be not deceived, and ye turn aside, and serve other gods, and worship them. **Deut. 11:16**

While the whole tone of this chapter is spiritual, still an x-ray is in order: what is your inmost, *personal* mind and heart response to what God says about womanhood as opposed to what the world says? Our mortal being naturally focuses upon and exalts self—so the message of the world strongly appeals. Our flesh doesn't like the idea of being Number Two in any way. But wait. The Bible tells us that God does all things well, so the assignment of roles is His *good* work. We're in a secondary position for the sake of overall order and efficient functioning. God constructed maleness for leading and femaleness for following. Masculine and feminine strengths differ; so do their weaknesses. As we carry out our divinely assigned roles, church, society, and families can function smoothly and effectively. We're also in a secondary position for the sake of wholeness. Gender-related innate strong and weak points are intended to mesh like the cogs on interlocking gears. Our roles and our beings complement each other. Too, our secondary place to man is a place of honor, provision, and protection. Genuine femininity inspires masculine respect. And our "weaker vessel" status encourages our men to provide our need for food, shelter, and so forth and to act as our protectors. Do you *resent* all that, or do you *rejoice* in it?

In approaching the study of beautiful femininity, what is your motive? Think about it honestly. As you consider possible improvement, if you were to put "physical" and "spiritual" on opposing arms of a scale, which would be heavier, and thus indicate your greater interest? Motive is "what makes us tick" in any given situation. If your motivation is to "upgrade" yourself *for* yourself or for human attention and approval, you need a major adjustment of heart and mind. If, however, you desire to be excellent and to do excellently as a servant of Jesus Christ, God will honor your efforts. Motives can be disguised—not only to others but also to ourselves. The most effective way to discern our motives is to present them to God:

> Search me, O God, and know my heart: try me, and know my thoughts: and see if there be any wicked way in me, and lead me in the way everlasting. **Ps. 139:23–24**

An encouragement as you move forward—whatever your temperament, personality, age, or profession, living a consistent Christian life in a dark world is tough. Nor is any one of us capable of success in our own strength. The glorious reality, however, is that success is possible in and through Him whom we love and serve. As you move on into the various areas of consideration found in the chapters ahead, do so strengthened in mind and spirit by the infusion of Philippians 2:13–15:

> For it is God which worketh in you both to will and to do of his good pleasure. Do all things without murmurings and disputings: that ye may be blameless and harmless, the sons of God, without rebuke, in the midst of a crooked and perverse nation, among whom ye shine as lights in the world.

Generation Considerations

Teens

Let no man despise thy youth; but be thou an example of the believers, in word, in conversation, in charity, in spirit, in faith, in purity. ***I Tim. 4:12***

Note particularly, please, the Scripture passages presented in this opening chapter and throughout the book. You teenagers often receive urgings and arguments that you shrug off as being just opinions and preferences of an older generation. Instead of shrugging, let some very important facts sink into your mind: those adults seeking to direct you are given by God to be your authorities, and they want your best. But don't simply give in to their wishes, keeping your contrary thoughts to yourself. Get into the Scripture yourself. Search it honestly and prayerfully. Maintain a heart that consistently seeks *God's* way rather than your way.

Mothers

That our daughters may be as corner stones, polished after the similitude of a palace. **Ps. 144:12**

Directing your children through the rough waters of their teenage years doesn't begin when they reach thirteen but at birth. Your daughter needs to see and sense the spiritual underpinnings of your life from the earliest times of her awareness. Your attitude toward the Bible will either help lay a solid foundation for your child, or it will give her nothing but the shifting sand of human opinion upon which to build her life. The talk of faith is cheap; the walk of faith is expensive. It will, of course, be the latter upon which your daughter focuses and from which she learns. As she observes you twenty-four hours a day, does she see biblical beauty?

Mentors

Showing to the generation to come the praises of the Lord, and his strength, and his wonderful works that he hath done. **Ps. 78:4**

Whether or not you have children or grandchildren of your own, you bear an important responsibility for mentoring. Christian mothers are having a tough time swimming upstream against the cultural rapids; they need your encouragement. Girls in their teens need someone outside the home to care about them and to supplement their training by modeling godly living in an ungodly world.

Caution Lights

Take heed therefore that the light which is in thee be not darkness. **Luke 11:35**

Every Christian home must have rules, and broken rules must have penalties. But discipline should be marked by a balance between mercy and truth. God always maintains that balance in His dealings with us, His children. There are two subtle "out-of-balance" dangers with regard to rules that can sabotage Christian parental training:

- saying or inferring that every rule is scriptural
- equating preferences with Scripture

It's also easy to get badly out of balance in the matter of modeling male/female life roles in the home. God never *denigrates* womanhood, or implies that women are inferior. He never intimates that they should be mindless automatons. The assignment of complementary roles is a functional one that facilitates order. Too, while the Bible's assignment puts considerable challenge and responsibility before women, it puts even more before men: according to Scripture, men are to live, love, and lead *as did Jesus Christ*!

The spirit of a home plays an indescribably important part in a child's formation. One regretful spirit of molding that has become evident in recent years is that which rears a daughter exclusively as a "breeder." She's taught (or it's inferred) that marriage and children are to be her life goal. Not so! *Of course* every girl should learn practical housework and food preparation skills. But if that's the capstone of home training, sad consequences may lie ahead. For every child God entrusts to us, the core aim in his or her training should be *personal love for God and finding and doing His will.* God does not intend every woman to marry. Rearing a girl to think He does can turn her aside from the purpose for which He really designed her. It can also make for frustration and bitterness in singleness rather than fulfillment, joyfulness, and effectiveness.

One final caution. The matter of womanly submission can be horribly distorted—even to the monstrous extreme of enduring abuse. There are wife-beaters who quote Scripture while they're making a punching bag of their spouse. A woman has no obligation to endure mistreatment. An abusive husband is not only violating God's law but also violating man's laws. Even before marriage there are some young men who twist the submission principle: they tell a girlfriend that she needs to "practice submission" in their dating relationship. Wrong! Before marriage she is not under his authority at all.

Most of what God has recorded for us in the Bible focuses upon our internal, spiritual self. The pages are filled with instruction, challenge, and rebuke. Our heavenly Father wants our *soul* to be pleasing to Him. As we bring our inmost being into conformity to His Word, our outer being—

which houses our gender distinction—will delight in His relatively few gender-specific teachings. So it is that the Lord urges us to

> *keep thy heart with all diligence; for out of it are the issues of life.*
> **Prov. 4:23**

Clearly, when there's something amiss in our concept and demonstration of femininity, the problem originates in our heart. A godly heart is not a weak, colorless thing: it is strong, discerning, faithful, and pure. It gives a girl or woman an iridescence of life that comes only from God's light.

CHAPTER THREE

Highlighting the Basics

CHapTer THree

Highlighting the Basics

The entrance of thy words giveth light; it giveth understanding unto the simple. **Ps. 119:130**

Throughout this book we're going to be focusing, of course, on you—you as a whole person who has the privilege and responsibility to reflect Jesus Christ. Reflect. That word could remind us of a gem—a precious stone whose facets reflect light. Interestingly, the Bible expresses that very concept:

And they shall be mine, saith the Lord of hosts, in that day when I make up my jewels. **Mal. 3:17**

Our value lies in what Christ has done for us: taken that which is only a lump of earth and transformed us into jewels.

Do you think of yourself as a gem? Each of us has a concept of self as a part of our human awareness. It colors our attitudes and our actions. Pride in oneself should not characterize a Christian. The apostle Paul reminded believers in Rome that no one was

to think of himself more highly than he ought to think; but to think soberly, according as God hath dealt to every man the measure of faith. **Rom. 12:3**

More often than pride, however, there seems to be a basic molecule in the female composition that persistently maintains negativism toward self.

Let's go back to Paul. In his letters to the churches, the apostle openly discusses his own blessings and his banes, his privileges and his pressures, his triumphs and his tears. Ultimately, he simply relinquished personal claim to all of what he was, what he did, what he'd experienced, and what he accomplished. That simple, profound, and exemplary reality is revealed in a beautiful little phrase,

> *by the grace of God I am what I am.* **I Cor. 15:10**

Our own concept of self would be balanced and healthy if we would—genuinely—operate from that same basis of surrender. Instead, we're natural experts in sensing—and dwelling upon—personal attributes or physical features that we consider inferior. The dissatisfaction reaches its zenith in the teen years, but it continues to be present throughout a woman's life.

Much of our struggle in the matter of self-concept is yearning for a capacity or stature of self that will make us capable to handle everything life sends us. But think how certainly we would then *glory* in our self-contained sufficiency! Our shortfall in self-concept, then, can actually benefit us spiritually if it brings us to acknowledge the reality of II Corinthians 3:5—

> *Not that we are sufficient of ourselves to think any thing as of ourselves; but our sufficiency is of God.*

Moreover, God reminds us in Jeremiah 9:23–24 of the littleness of those things we would like to be or to have—

> *Thus saith the Lord, Let not the wise man glory in his wisdom, neither let the mighty man glory in his might, let not the rich man glory in his riches: but let him that glorieth glory in this, that he understandeth and knoweth me, that I am the Lord which exercise lovingkindness, judgment, and righteouness, in the earth: for in these things I delight, saith the Lord.*

Accurate personal evaluation for a Christian really is relaxation into God-ward trust.

- We trust God's perfect wisdom and love in creating every part of ourselves.
- We trust His perfect wisdom and love for healing and beautifying our hurts.

- We trust His perfect wisdom and love to supply whatever we may lack in ourselves as we seek to live for Him.

It's far better to be a God-made, God-reflecting gem than to be a self-made, self-proclaiming faux jewel!

No gem comes into its full potential without cutting and polishing; not even the finest palace comes into being without planning and labor. So it is with each of us who desires to be her best for Jesus Christ.

Physical health provides the stable underpinnings for beauty. It is essential to give attention to our body's condition throughout life. Meticulous grooming, knowledgeable use of cosmetics and clothing, graceful carriage, impeccable manners, and pleasing speech—all are wasted in effort and effect if we overlook matters of nutrition and good health. While we recognize that our physical frame is flawed, temporal, and not of primary focus, we must also remember two Scripture truths:

- Our body is God's creation and thus a stewardship responsibility.

For thou hast possessed my reins: thou hast covered me in my mother's womb. I will praise thee; for I am fearfully and wonderfully made: marvellous are thy works; and that my soul knoweth right well. My substance was not hid from thee, when I was made in secret, and curiously wrought in the lowest parts of the earth. Thine eyes did see my substance, yet being unperfect; and in thy book all my members were written, which in continuance were fashioned, when as yet there was none of them. **Ps. 139:13–16**

- Our body is the temple of the Holy Spirit, thus making its care a spiritual responsibility.

Know ye not that ye are the temple of God, and that the Spirit of God dwelleth in you? If any man defile the temple of God, him shall God destroy; for the temple of God is holy, which temple ye are. **I Cor. 3:16–17**

Physical Health

For no man ever yet hated his own flesh; but nourisheth and cherisheth it, even as the Lord the church. **Eph. 5:29**

It is impossible to look your best if you don't feel well. No matter how busy and demanding your life, Christian woman, good health should be foundational in your self-care. If you have a family, of course, that principle most certainly applies in your provision for them! A husband and children greatly broaden your health-focused responsibilities.

It's amazing to me that any medical doctor can complete the study and conduct the care of the human body but still believe it results from evolution. The body as a whole, as well as any of its separate parts, wonderfully proclaims its Maker. What a marvelous creation the human body is—yet how careless even we Christians may become in tending it. Those of us who have a personal heart relationship with the God who created our bodies should responsibly tend them as part of our honor and service for Him.

Food and Nutrition

Who giveth food to all flesh: for his mercy endureth for ever. **Ps. 136:25**

Old Testament dietary laws were not just a formality; they were a means whereby God mounted a health guard for His people. The ancient Greeks recognized definite connections between health and food. They perceived that food is the source of physical building material, and they recommended certain foods for certain physical benefits. Only in the late eighteenth century, however, was the science of nutrition born. The study began through observing and trying to prevent diseases—specifically malaria, scurvy, and beri beri. Then in the nineteenth and early twentieth century came the concept of energy metabolism and essential nutrients.

We who live in the twenty-first century can be thankful for the abundant information we have available in the area of nutrition. Only a hermit could claim ignorance. We also live in a land of unparalleled bounty, where all sorts of foods are available to us year-round. So, except for cases of extreme poverty, failure to eat wisely comes down to just two things: irresponsibility and self-indulgence.

Abundance of information can also be confusing because claims, counterclaims, and changing claims in the field of nutrition appear regularly. The best way to chart a safe course through it all is with common sense: know the basics of how the human body uses food, know what it requires for optimum health, and know any individual condition(s) you have that may demand extra attention.

My Encyclopedia Britannica entry on digestion covers more than six pages, each page having two columns, and with the information written in small print. Obviously, only a distillation can be given here. But a thumbnail sketch of our physical system's intricate operation helps remind us of God's creative finesse.

Digestion is what our body does in taking food, changing it to liquid, and absorbing it for use. The foods we ingest contain proteins, carbohydrates, and fats. The digestive process, which we generally take for granted, actually is an intricate operation. (I had to shake my head over humanity's determined rejection of creationism in reading the encyclopedia account because there were several comments about digestion's mysteries and how such intricacies had "evolved.") Food's digestive path of course begins in the mouth, where we chew and swallow; then it moves by means of peristalsis (wavelike contractions) through the esophagus, stomach, and small intestine, with waste going on into the large intestine. Absorption into the body takes place almost entirely in the small intestine. From the moment food enters our mouth, it is broken down into usable form by digestive secretions: saliva, gastric juice, pancreatic juice, intestinal secretions, and bile.

Food is much more than just something that pleases our taste buds and satisfies hunger. It fuels every function of our body. A healthy diet is essential to a positive physical energy quotient, to effective mental activity, and to a pleasing appearance. Conversely, poor eating habits can weaken the body, short-circuit the mind, and decimate physical attractiveness.

Solid nutrition facts are established only over time as they're tested on large numbers of subjects and with a wide range of contributing factors taken into account. Beware of food fads. Eating plans that don't provide a balance of nutrients can damage health. Particularly to be avoided are one-food or one-food-group diet recommendations.

Unfortunately, the fast pace of modern life is leaving an ever-broader trail of physical and mental maladies; we have established careless grab-a-bite food intake patterns. American families have fallen into many eating habits that detract from optimum health physically, emotionally, and even relationally. Some of those include the following:

- skipping breakfast
- eating an on-the-run, high-carbohydrate, high-sugar breakfast
- having a fast-food lunch of high-fat foods and high-sugar beverages
- supplementing between meals with sugary, fatty, or salty snacks
- eating a fragmented evening meal
- not sitting down together as a family
- individuals resorting to various frozen entrees popped into the microwave oven

Just reading that list exposes the weakness and failure of our fuel intake. Obviously, then, we need to ponder the matter. Wise eating habits are an important part of responsible physical stewardship.

Beginning in the 1990s, Americans have been pointed to a "food pyramid" established by the USDA (United States Department of Agriculture) as the standard for healthful eating. Then in 2001 the Harvard Medical School established a new food pyramid, detailing the errors and weaknesses in the USDA model. The restructured pyramid looks like this:

Healthy Eating Pyramid

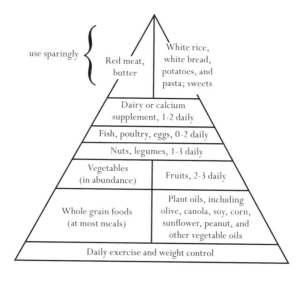

As you study the food pyramid, recognize that nutrition is just one aspect of a healthy overall lifestyle. Various sources recommend the following health-enhancing practices:

- Watch your weight. Medical experts increasingly warn that being overweight is a key health enemy. (Weight-loss information will be presented in the next chapter.)
- Opt for good fats rather than bad fats (saturated and trans fats). Olive oil is particularly beneficial.
- Get your carbohydrates from whole grains.
- Eat less red meat. Recognize soy as a good protein source as well as nuts and nut butters and fish from cold waters (salmon, tuna, sardines, and so forth).
- Eat plenty of vegetables and fruits. Leafy dark greens are best; potatoes should be a rarity. Berries are excellent as antioxidants (especially blueberries, blackberries, strawberries, and raspberries).
- Consider drinking water an essential part of every day (ideally, eight glasses per day).
- Take a good multivitamin to supplement your diet.
- Reduce sugar intake (read labels even of unsuspected products).
- Reduce salt intake.
- Exercise regularly.

There are also some special considerations for women. For instance, we need more iron (particularly in premenopausal years) and calcium than men. Iron deficiency anemia may be characterized by weakness, fatigue, and headaches. Women need calcium because we are more susceptible to osteoporosis (loss of bone density) than men; weakened bones break easily. We should be particularly careful about our intake of fats; there is increasing evidence that bad fats not only contribute to high cholesterol but to breast cancer as well.

All of my reading emphasized the importance of adequate water intake. Experts say that by the time we're thirsty, our body is probably already partially dehydrated. Water is a key part of the human body, both in its makeup and in its operation. More than half of the body's water is contained in tissue cells—that is, cells of our bones, muscles, blood, and fat. The rest of the water is between cells—as in our eyes and our joints. The body also uses water in its various fluids and functions: to move glucose to the muscles, to remove metabolic waste matter from the body, to dissolve chemical compounds, and to house necessary chemical reactions. No wonder it's so important to drink plenty of water every day!

Careful attention to and choice of healthful foods can be nullified by poor preparation methods. Most healthy cooking principles are simple, and we know them; but do we apply the knowledge? For example, frying (and certainly deep-fat frying) adds fat to food; so do creamy sauces, margarine, and butter. Rich dressings can cancel out a tossed salad's low-calorie, high-vitamin benefits. Boiled veggies lose flavor and nutrients to the water; it's better to steam them. Overcooking by any method can destroy nutritional value. And always consider using low-fat products in recipes; they're now readily available.

If you've been neglectful in the matter of nutrition, be encouraged to know that your eating habits are exactly that—habits; they can be changed. You can also retrain your tastes. None of that will come instantly—but perseverance will eventually pay off, and you'll come to prefer healthy foods.

Sleep and Rest

And he said unto them, Come ye yourselves apart into a desert place, and rest a while: for there were many coming and going, and they had no leisure so much as to eat. **Mark 6:31**

That Bible description of life's hectic pace and its pressure sounds contemporary, doesn't it? And for many of us it's quite accurate. Does Jesus drive His disciples to keep at it unstintingly? Not at all. He accommodates their need for rest. God Himself rested in the days of creation. He built into the Law one full day for rest out of every seven. And He so constructed our bodies that they require renewal through regular sleep periods.

There are individual variations in sleep requirements, but most people need six to eight hours of sleep each night. Too, women generally need more sleep than men.

Just as we often operate with unwise food intake, we also tend to violate sleep needs. Researchers have noted that Americans now sleep one and a half hours less than they did a hundred years ago. "Tired" is a descriptive word heard far too often in our modern society. Sleep deprivation has a number of negative results. Among them are the following:

- lowered energy
- impaired muscle growth and repair
- greater susceptibility to colds and flu
- memory impairment
- difficulty in learning
- weakened emotional control
- increase in negative moods

There were also two particularly insightful and unexpected findings from the studies: lack of sleep increased appetite for starchy foods, candy, and salty snacks. Also, the more tired people became, the more confident they were that they were not exhibiting any impairment.

It's important to know and honor your personal sleep requirements. They reflect a part of God's creative touch: they're boundaries within which you're to operate for best results. A body that's consistently driven beyond its sleep-need boundaries will eventually experience damage of one sort or another. It's also important to provide for *quality* sleep. That doesn't mean sleeping pills. (They can create increasing dependency.) It does mean darkness, quiet, a good mattress, and avoiding stimulants near bedtime.

If yours is the kind of life that often finds you skimping on a full night's sleep, learn to compensate with a daily nap. The term "power nap" has come into usage because of the benefits derived. Some great men of the past also credited napping for their level of accomplishment. Among them were Winston Churchill, Thomas Edison, Albert Einstein, and Napoleon Bonaparte. Latin countries have traditionally practiced afternoon naps.

The napping habit can be a tremendous contributor to body, brain, relationships, accomplishment, and efficiency. For women who work professionally, napping may offer a challenge or even seem impossible. Encouragingly, though, some organizations, recognizing the heightened effectiveness of rested employees, are providing nap rooms. Too, what about the couch in the ladies lounge? Or you might even effectively return to an elementary school practice—putting your head down on your desk. Even a very few minutes of mind-on-nothing, physically relaxed rest can benefit your entire day and being. Using your break for a nap would be far better than wasting it in the break room or in idle gossip on the telephone.

Don't dismiss the idea of napping with "I'm too busy" or "I can't sleep in the daytime." Busyness easily and often becomes just nonproductive motion when we're tired. Give yourself several weeks on the project, and you can train yourself to nap. Think in terms of only ten to twenty minutes. Napping longer than thirty minutes in the daytime is not recommended; it tends to leave you groggy and may make it difficult to fall asleep at night.

Skimping on sleep not only shows up today in dark-circled eyes and dragging steps, but it also makes a hefty deposit today toward tomorrow's premature aging. In fact, sleep studies have discovered that the negative effects of missed sleep are normally characteristic of aging itself.

Exercise

She girdeth her loins with strength, and strengtheneth her arms. **Prov. 31:17**

We may tend to think that only folks who want to lose weight or excel in sports need exercise. Not so. In essence, exercise is a general life enhancer. Vigorous exercise used to be a built-in component of daily existence, not just for men out working in the fields but also for women keeping their homes.

Note that the Harvard Medical School's healthy-eating pyramid combines daily exercise and weight control as its *base*. Modern America's sedentary lifestyle—and its many negative effects—presents major concerns to health professionals. For many of us females, especially, exercise is a nasty word when it refers to deliberate, regular, strenuous activity, though it has been proven to make multiple contributions to the body's well-being. Exercise helps maintain healthy cardiovascular and pulmonary systems. It strengthens and tones muscles. It contributes to positive bone density. It aids flexibility and balance. How does it do all that? Through a simple physiological process: *stress correctly applied enhances strength*.

A Christian woman certainly should consider strength to be an important characteristic in her physical self, just as it is in her spiritual self. Exercise benefits her bodily temple in its operation, its production, and its testimony.

The Bible tells us that a wise person thinks ahead; he doesn't heedlessly rush into things (Prov. 22:3; 27:12). Before beginning an exercise program, it's prudent to go to your doctor to have him evaluate your health. There are of course some physical conditions that require special limitations in exercise or that require a particularly gradual approach in undertaking it.

A good exercise program addresses different facets and functions of your physical self: aerobics to benefit heart, lungs, circulation, and general stamina; stretches and lifts to maintain skeletal flexibility and muscle strength. And both types of exercise positively affect bone strength and density. Most women can't afford an hour a day for exercise. But all can invest twenty to thirty minutes. The key, of course, is a combination of desire, determination, and discipline. There are many exercise choices available. Consider just a few suggestions.

Aerobics	Stretches and Lifts
walking	sit-ups
jogging	push-ups/chin-ups
step routines	toe-touches
swimming	parallel lunges
biking	deep-knee bends
jumping rope	free weights

There are also technological "companions" and encouragers available—for example, treadmills, weight machines, and stationary bikes and exercise routines played through your television set. I highly recommend the exercise videos produced by Linda Haught (available through BJU Press) because of their gradation, their thoroughness, and their good music.

Exercise not only results in the obvious physical health enhancements; it has other, more subtle benefits as well. It clears the mind of cobwebs. It calms emotions and contributes to a sense of well-being. I've found that it even helps to keep my sinuses clear. And, finally, it encourages more fluid intake and less food intake.

Common sense needs to be operational when exercising. For instance, don't eat immediately before you exercise. Drink plenty of water before, during, and afterwards. If you have warning symptoms such as chest pain, nausea, or lightheadedness, go back to see your doctor.

We adults aren't the only ones who need to build exercise into our lives. Obesity in children is becoming a major health concern: active childhood has been replaced by TV-watching, video-game-playing, snacks-consuming inactivity. Then when those children become adults, machines and technological gadgets coddle—and further fatten—them by taking away the need for much physical effort.

Parents must see to it that children are physically active: turn off the TV and quit buying video games. Get the kids out in the yard to *play*—running, jumping, climbing, and so forth. For our own inactivity, we can counteract the stultifying effect of technology by backing away from constant reliance upon its products. Go toward greater physical exertion throughout every day.

- Wash and dry dishes by hand.
- Use a heavy vacuum cleaner instead of a lightweight one.
- Care for your lawn with a push mower instead of a riding mower.
- Run, skip, and jump occasionally as you go about your housework.
- Walk instead of driving whenever possible.
- Teens, sign up for that sport, class, or outside activity that demands exercise.
- Use stairs instead of elevators and escalators.

- Park as far from the store as possible, instead of looking for that close spot.
- Wash your car by hand instead of running it through a car wash.
- Take your dog for several turns around the block.

Most of us recognize that our mindset makes a tremendous difference in any endeavor. We can apply that attitude-adjustment principle to the matter of exercise. Simply by changing from an "oh, no!" attitude toward physical exertion to "ah, yes!" we can begin to move toward more healthy lives. And as in the matter of nutrition, so too in exercise: our change of attitude and action needs to be a *lifetime* change—not just a temporary thing. We can certainly claim the Lord's help in keeping us active for the sake of His Spirit's dwelling place.

Just as in our spiritual life, so too in our physical life, the surface considerations are really only significant and worthwhile if the inner, or foundational, matters are sound. So aim for good health—it's foundational to beauty.

General Grooming

A living translation of "good grooming" would be "clean, neat, and attractive." The two last-named characteristics, neat and attractive, can't be a reality unless first there's cleanliness. Just as reputable merchants make sure that the windows in which they display their goods are well washed, so we who seek to direct attention to our lovely Lord must be consistently careful about cleanliness: *the Christian girl or woman should be an attractive show-window for her Lord.* There is absolutely no excuse for a dirty Christian! God through His prophet Isaiah challenges:

Be ye clean, that bear the vessels of the Lord. **Isa. 52:11**

We who are saved don't just bear the vessels of the Lord; we *are* His vessels since the Holy Spirit dwells within us. Too, Old Testament ritual entailed cleansing of the animal sacrifice and of the priest who offered the sacrifice. The apostle Paul in the New Testament exhorts the believer:

Present your bodies a living sacrifice. **Rom. 12:1**

How can we possibly imagine such a yielded one being unclean?

Cleanliness is fundamental to any discussion of personal appearance. If you are not scrupulously *clean* about your person and clothing, your interest in, effort toward, or program for self-improvement will be doomed to failure.

Specifically, scour-and-polish efforts need to be exerted upon all our physical "surfaces"—skin, hair, nails, teeth, and clothing.

Skin

Sometimes we seem to take thoughtful care only of the skin on our faces. And yet skin covers our entire earthly tabernacle, and all of it needs careful tending. Skin is, in fact, the largest of the body's organs, and one of its strategic functions is elimination: it carries off waste by means of its sweat glands and pores. Skin also shields us against external damaging elements such as bacteria, chemicals, and ultraviolet rays. Too, it regulates body temperature and makes us aware of touch, pressure, and pain. Obviously, the much-abused, taken-for-granted, water-proofing "hide" we carry around is actually an intricate part of God's human creation.

The obvious, visible part of the skin is known as the epidermis. It's made up of dying and dead cells that are being constantly replaced with new cells produced beneath it. Under the epidermis is the dermis. It houses the skin's "factory"—nerve endings, blood vessels, sebaceous (oil) glands, sweat glands, and collagen fibers. The latter render the skin resilient and strong. The deepest skin layer is the hypodermis. It is mainly a cushion of fat cells for our blood, lymph, and nervous systems; it also helps preserve our body heat. If God's concern in creating us was so minutely detailed as is evidenced in our skin structure and functions, shouldn't our skin care be more painstaking?

Body Skin Care

Keep your skin—all of it—*clean.* That means thorough cleansing at least once a day. Of course, you wash your hands many times a day—as, for instance, at the end of *every* bathroom visit. And strenuous activity or excessive heat demands another shower or bath. The skin's vital elimination work produces a distinctive, unpleasant aroma. It's the well-advertised (and self-advertising) "B.O."—body odor.

All of your skin is working and leaving odor-producing deposits. So a dab of deodorant here, a splash of cologne there, will *not* create aromatic sweetening! The only way to conquer odor is to remove its cause: in other words, wash off the skin's secretions. A loofa sponge can be a particularly effective bath or shower item. Daily cleansing with soap and water is available to, inexpensive for, and *demanded of* any woman who desires to represent the Lord Jesus and draw people to Him.

Some places on the body demand special cleaning attention. They are areas where structure or enclosure worsen odor problems:

- feet
- underarms
- genital area

All these must be thoroughly washed at least once daily, *and* deodorized as needed. For such problem areas, it's not a matter of "either-or"—deodorants and antiperspirants are a must.

Individual bodies respond differently to deodorant and antiperspirant products. It may take you quite a while to find the brand or formula that's best for you. Also, sometimes one formula temporarily loses its effectiveness. It's as if you become immune to its working. When that happens, change from what you've been using. Eventually, you may be able to return to your original preference.

The female menstrual cycle complicates odor problems. When you're having your period, take extra, careful precautions against offensive odor. There are also other times when vaginal discharge may cause odor problems. Be aware! There are special deodorizing products available for these problems.

Some areas of the body need special attention because of their particular operation, exposure, or pressure-bearing function:

- hands
- knees
- elbows
- heels

Skin in these areas may demand extra cleansing efforts against ground-in dirt and discoloration. For example, if your elbows have darkened, try using lemon juice on them once a week.

A final consideration in overall skin hygiene is the regular removal of hair from underarms and legs. *Hairiness is unacceptable for a lady in America.* There are several ways to remove unwanted body hair, and each technique has specific characteristics and recommendations for safety and effectiveness.

Shaving. For legs and underarms. This is the simplest, fastest, and cheapest. Hair is cut off at the surface of the skin. There may be a slight sensation of scratching. Smooth skin after shaving generally lasts from one to three days. *Usage notes:* Soap lather or shaving gel helps the razor glide more smoothly. Dull blades can scratch and pull skin, so it's a good idea to replace blades often. (Recommendations range from after three shaves to after six.) Of course it's important to use a razor carefully in order to avoid nicks and cuts. Do not shave if skin is broken or irritated. Don't shave over the same spot more than a couple of times. In the underarm area hair doesn't grow in just one direction; the best shaving technique is to shave up first, then down.

Depilatories. For legs and underarms. Creams and gels containing a chemical called calcium thioglycolate dissolve the hair to just below the skin's surface. Removal of hair may take from five to fifteen minutes. Depilatory products are improving in their rather unpleasant smell. There may be a tingling sensation where hair has been removed. Hair doesn't grow back for two to five days. *Usage notes:* It's wise to test the product on a small patch of skin for allergic or sensitivity reactions; wait twenty-four hours for the test to be complete. Depilatories can burn the skin if left on too long or used too often.

Waxing. For legs. Wax is applied on hair in the direction of its growth, then pulled off in the direction opposite from growth, removing hair by the roots. Users report that it feels like adhesive tape being pulled off skin. Hair grows back in two to six weeks. *Usage notes:* Waxing may leave small red bumps. (Usually, they're the denuded skin saying "ouch!") Never wax over varicose veins, moles, warts, irritated or broken skin, or sunburn.

Removal of facial hair will be discussed later in the chapter.

This important protective note can be an effective bridge between considerations of body skin to those of facial skin: for both, *take great care to avoid sun damage.* Summer sun's bronze can very easily lead to early or excessive wrinkling, and even to skin cancer. And when you think "sunburn," put emphasis on the "burn," thus reminding yourself of its seriousness and potential damage. Anytime you're going to be in the sun, put a moisturizing, ultra-violet-shielding lotion on your skin. Doctors are alarmed by the rapidly increasing incidences of skin cancers as people insist upon tanning.

Facial Care

Now we come to that particular skin-covered patch that looks back at us in mirrors large or small: our face. As with the rest of the body, here too the basic care principle to be observed is *cleanliness.* No matter how a protester might back-pedal or bluster, *clogged pores are not lovely, and blackheads are not beauty marks!*

Our skin can be adversely affected by a number of different factors: wind and sun, medications, temperature extremes, poor diet, hormonal changes, stress, and air pollution.

Generally speaking, by their thirties women recognize the importance of good skin care. However, they may simultaneously discover that they must pay for youth's carelessness. Ideally, a girl should learn good skin-cleansing habits as soon as she's old enough to hold a washcloth. Her washcloth and mild glycerin or castile soap or similar water-soluble cleanser is probably all she'll need until she's in her twenties. Some young women, though, have to go the extra mile in skin care due to the onset of acne, eczema, or rashes. It's wise to seek a dermatologist's care for those special skin problems.

There are three basic skin types: dry, normal, and oily. Any one of the basic types may also be highly sensitive. There can be combined types on one face; for example, basically normal but with oily areas on forehead, nose, and chin. Each type has its own particular tendencies or problems.

Dry skin develops lines more easily than the other types because of low oil secretion. Normal skin may break out now and then, especially on the chin and nose. Normal skin can also become dry when not properly cared for. Oily skin is pimple-prone, and it is often further characterized by enlarged pores and blackheads. Sensitive skin is vulnerable to both external and internal influences such as irritants or allergens. Reactions may be flakiness, under-skin bumps, and swelling.

Each type of skin is best cared for with a three-step procedure: cleansing, toning, and moisturizing. The steps, though, should involve products differently formulated according to their skin friendliness.

Dry skin. Clean with a cream or rich liquid cleanser or with a moisturizing soap. Rinse thoroughly with warm water. Toner should be mild and alcohol-free. Cool water will also work. Pat with a towel to dry. Moisturize with an enriched cream, taking special care around eyes (where wrinkles typically first appear). *Special note:* Check all face products to guard against alcohol content.

Normal skin. This type can use liquid or cream cleansers, water-soluble cleanser, or gentle facial soap. Rinse with warm water. Toner may or may not contain alcohol. Moisturize with a light lotion or cream. *Special note:* If skin begins to show signs of dryness, change to nonalcohol toner. (Water hydrates the skin, but then it evaporates, leaving skin dryer than before. Thus, the need for moisturizer.)

Oily skin. Cleanser may be a light lotion or a milk cleanser. Treat skin eruptions with medicated cleanser. Rinse with warm water. An alcohol-based toner is effective for oily skin, but check to be sure the alcohol is not ethanol, methanol, or isopropyl. Nonoily, noncomedogenic (doesn't block pores) products are recommended. *Special note:* Don't use harsh cleansers or toners, and don't pick at or squeeze pimples and blackheads.

Sensitive skin. Cleanser should be hypoallergenic. Do not use soap. Choose alcohol-free or hypoallergenic toner. Moisturizer should also be hypoallergenic. *Special note:* A product *scent* may adversely affect this type of skin. Always do a product test on your skin, waiting twenty-four hours to check for possible reaction.

And, finally, some general reminders for all types of skin care:

- Be sure any cleansing product is thoroughly rinsed away. Remaining soap or cleanser film attracts dirt and may clog pores.
- Don't rub your face to dry it; pat dry with a soft towel.
- *Consider your neck to be part of your face in caring for your skin.* It can pay big dividends as you age.
- Toner (astringent or freshener) works to tighten pores after the cleansing and prepares it for moisturizer and makeup.
- An exfoliant scrub or mask used once a week removes dead cells that dull skin's surface.
- Alpha hydroxy acid complexes (AHAs) have the effect of a mini skin peel.
- All skin types are wise to use products containing sunscreen (noted by the letters SPF and a number indicating its protective strength).
- Be gentle with facial skin, not stretching or rubbing it vigorously.
- Take special care in cleaning around your eyes, where skin is particularly fragile. If you wear eye makeup, use a cream or liquid remover, and work with your third finger (rather than your index finger) or cotton swabs—never rubbing or dragging the skin.

At the end of a day when evening social activities lie ahead, if at all possible, don't fall into the trap of thinking "another coat of makeup will fix it." Start fresh! You'll not only look better but you'll also feel better after cleansing your face and redoing makeup.

Facial Hair

Female faces aren't really hairless, but facial hair is typically light and virtually invisible. Sometimes, though, there may be dark hairs that appear singly or in various-sized patches. There are several reasons for unwanted hair to appear on the face: genetics, hormonal variations, birth control pills, or a side effect of some medications. For most of us, it's just our eyebrows that are overly hairy. However, some must do battle with a moustache-like growth on the upper lip or a jaw line that's whiskery. *Never shave facial hair.* There is a varied arsenal of effective anti-facial-hair weapons.

The areas most commonly treated in women are eyebrows, upper lip, and chin.

Tweezing. Hairs are pulled out individually by the roots. Good tweezers and a magnifying mirror are the only equipment needed.

Depilatories. These must be specifically designated as suitable for facial use. Even so, be sure to do a skin test first.

Waxing. The technique is identical to that described in the earlier section on body hair. Experts recommend that waxing be done professionally because working with wax (especially around the eyes) can be difficult. *Usage note:* If you use Accutane, Retin-A, or Remova, *do not try waxing.* The top layer of skin may come off with the wax!

Electrolysis. A needle delivers low levels of electricity into hair follicles, killing the roots one by one. This technique is reportedly more painful than tweezing. When the treatment is repeated over several months for up to a year, hair never grows in again. *Usage note:* Electrolysis can leave scars and discolor skin if done incorrectly. Check to be sure the practitioner has passed the CPE (Certified Professional Electrologist) test and that she uses a separate needle for each client.

Threading. This is a new technique in America, imported from India and the Middle East. A length of cotton thread is twisted and rolled quickly across the skin, pulling hair out by the roots.

Laser. This technique is most effective in removing dark hair from light skin; lasers do not work well on white, gray, or very blonde hairs. After gel is applied, the instrument is passed over the area. Light is transmitted one to two millimeters into the skin. Converting to heat, the light damages the hair follicle. Regrowth of hair varies widely, as do descriptions of the pain involved.

Photo-epilation. Newly approved by the FDA (Food and Drug Administration), this method permanently removes hair. Intense light destroys the hair follicles. Tests have demonstrated 50–60 percent hair clearance in twelve weeks.

Hair Care

Jesus made a heart-warming statement about God's intimate love and care:

But the very hairs of your head are all numbered. **Matt. 10:30**

Human hairs are many: roughly 100,000 to 150,000 hair follicles cover our head, and each follicle grows about twenty new hairs in a lifetime. We're actually covered with hair except for our lips, palms, and soles of our feet. Hair follicles go through cycles of growth and rest. Those growth/rest/shedding cycles come at different times—otherwise, we would have periods of total hairlessness. Plucking a hair stimulates the follicle to grow another. As a person ages, the number of active hair follicles declines. Heredity and health contribute to the extent of hair loss, and hair health reflects nutrition.

There are many different types and colors of hair; each responds best to type-focused care and products. Each of the three major races has its own hair characteristics. Oriental hair is always black, and it is straight. Negroid hair is black and tightly curled. Caucasian hair ranges from curly to straight and from very pale blonde to black. Cross-sectioned and magnified hair reveals that the shape of the hair shaft itself differs from race to race. Oriental hair shafts are almost completely round, Negroid hairs are strongly oval with definite edges, and Caucasian hair shafts are usually oval but less defined at the edges. The curl variations come from structural distinctions, as well. Such structural details highlight two things: our great Creator's minute attention and the need for our using different methods of care.

Hair's appearance is important to both men and women. It serves as the frame for our face, and we know our face to be the two-way physical window through which we view the world and the world views us. The term "bad hair day" has real meaning. I was particularly interested to read one hair care expert's observation that men are more negatively affected by such a day than women are. Smile, ladies! Hair color strongly contributes to our overall facial color palette. More will be said about the latter in the chapter dealing with clothing choices.

Hair Care Products

We are both blessed and challenged by living at a time when there is a tremendous range and variety of hair care products available. We can thereby either benefit or be boggled. The basis for your choice of shampoo and conditioner should not be primarily brand or price—but your individual needs according to hair type and hair health. The aim, of course, is to have the *healthiest* hair possible. "Sick" hair can't be beautiful.

I gleaned in reading through many sources that the most effective way to make wise choices in the hair care department is to *read content labels*. What's in the product acts upon your hair either positively or negatively. But remember that despite expense and chemical wonders, externals are secondary to internals: healthy hair must have a protein-rich diet. High on a weight-conscious list as sources of protein would be tuna, salmon, cottage cheese, and chicken. Following is a sample of hair-care products' contents according to specific hair needs.

Growing or maintaining long hair	Hydrolized wheat proteins, wheat starch, amino acids, dimethicone or another silicone
Adding volume	Guar gum or vegetable proteins (preferably from soy or wheat), polyquaternium-10
Enhancing curls	Dimethicone or another silicone glycerin, and polyquaternium-10
Controlling frizz	Sesame
Protecting color	Betaines or amphodiacetates, and guar gum
Counteracting brassy tones	D and C violet #2
Straightening and smoothing	Dimethicone or other silicone, glycerin, hydrolyzed wheat proteins, polyquaternium-10
Moisturizing dry or damaged hair	Dimethicone or other alternate silicone, guar gum, hydrolyzed wheat proteins, vitamin E, aloe vera, panthenol, and ingredients with names ending in -onium

Combating dandruff	One of these six ingredients: pyrithione zinc, coal tar, selenium disulfide, piroctone olamine, salicylic acid, ketoconazole, or sulfur

A further note about labels: ingredients are listed from highest concentration to lowest. Also look to be sure the label indicates that the product is pH balanced. And don't opt for baby shampoos: not only do they lack pH balance but they're also intended primarily for scalp cleansing, not hair health.

Although one shampoo may give you good results for years, be aware that hair, like skin, changes with the passage of time. Typical changes involve lightening color and increasing fragility, some thinning of the hair, and drying scalp. You should then, of course, look for a shampoo with the contents that will address the problem.

Besides the daily and relatively minor hair challenges just mentioned, there is the more serious problem of hair loss. If you should notice loss of hair greater than you normally shed, be aware of what it may mean. The following information can be helpful at such a time.

Brittleness, breakage, and some loss	Probably caused by use of curling or straightening irons, hot rollers, tight braiding, or repeated use of chemicals on the hair.
Coin-sized or larger bald patches that are smooth and round	Usually beginning in childhood, this indicates an autoimmune disease in which the immune system attacks hair-growth cells.
Bald spot(s) with abnormal scalp appearance	Indicates a systemic infection, autoimmune disease, scalp trauma (e.g., injury or burn), or radiation therapy.
Sudden overall hair loss by handsful	May result from childbirth, surgery, crash or starvation diets, drug reactions, or severe emotional distress.

Persistent and chronic overall loss	This can be brought on by a protein deficiency (as in an eating disorder), iron-deficiency anemia, thyroid or hormonal disorder.

Hair Care Techniques and Tips

Before shampooing. Get all tangles out of your hair by a good brushing session. Brushing loosens surface dirt and stimulates the scalp. Shampooing can break hairs if tangles haven't been removed. I had that fact *painfully* proven when a time crunch forced me to go to a beautician other than the one who regularly cuts my hair. She popped my head into the sink with no prebrushing, and the tearing hairs not only hurt; I could even hear their death struggles!

Experts advise that the brush itself is important; they recommend brushes with natural boar bristles. Natural bristles are less likely to cause breakage and they're more efficient in distributing natural oils from roots to ends of hair. The diameter of a brush should be larger for long hair, and very thick hair may need a brush with combined natural and synthetic bristles. A round brush can help create volume, and a paddle-shape brush is best for smoothing. A session of gentle brushing at night can stimulate growth in thinning hair. However, there's no need for the hundred-strokes brushing routine our grandmothers may have recommended. It can have negative effects. According to historians, that extended brushing routine began long ago as a battle plan against head lice.

Shampooing. Hair care professionals are moving away from once-a-day shampoo recommendations. They now suggest every-other day or even every-third-day shampoos. The reason is that hair looks and responds its natural best when the oils from the scalp are allowed to reach all the way to the ends of the hairs. Excess washing damages hair by counteracting the needed lubrication. You may also be using too much shampoo each time. The "less is more" principle should apply.

It's also wise to pull back from the lather-twice habit. One source pointed out that a shampoo manufacturer first recommended the practice, for obvious reasons: increased sales. But a single lathering is sufficient un-less hair is unusually dirty. (Note that shampoo labels now usually omit the lather-twice line, or they recommend following the shampoo with a moisturizing treatment.) If you have a problem with product buildup on your hair, try a clarifying shampoo every two weeks.

When shampooing, use the tips of your fingers—not your fingernails. Your scalp needs massaging action rather than scratching.

While you're shampooing, your brushes and combs can be freshening up, too. Don't use dirty instruments on clean hair. Soak them in a sink full of sudsy water, then rinse while your hair is wrapped in a towel or is air-drying.

Make one more thing a habit as you shampoo: washing your ears. Use a cloth to clean them as thoroughly as possible during the shampoo, then finish the job with a cotton swab sometime during the drying process.

Rinsing. Most published sources recommend using a need-specific mois-turizer after each shampoo. The product should be thoroughly worked through the hair (concentrating on coverage of the ends) and then rinsed out immediately. There are, however, some moisturizers that work best if left in slightly longer. Read the label. African-American women's hair re-sponds best to conditioners containing jojoba or coconut oil.

Thorough rinsing is a must. The old term "squeaky clean" still holds as a standard. Rinsing should be finished off with water as *cool* as you can stand it. Cool water seals the hair's cuticle and makes the hair shaft smooth and shiny.

Towel drying. Rough drying with a towel can damage hair. Protective recommendations urge squeezing out excess water by hand, then patting dry or wrapping with a towel.

Detangling. Here's another juncture where hair is susceptible to dam-age. Use a big-tooth comb and work carefully from the ends to the roots rather than vice versa. If your hair loves to hold on to its snarls when wet, apply a leave-in detangling product, then comb.

Blow-drying. With the preceding emphasis on hair's need to retain its natural oils for health, common sense should conclude that there are dangers to avoid in blow-drying. Specific warnings are in order. *Do not* blow-dry dripping wet hair. It's best to wrap your head in a towel for about five minutes, then let hair air-dry for at least another five minutes. At that point you would apply your setting lotion, mousse, or spritz as needed. Hair should be only slightly damp when you begin the blow dry. Use a dryer setting no higher than medium, don't hold the nozzle too close to your head while drying (less than an eight-to-ten-inch distance), and don't apply the heat longer than a total of twenty minutes.

Styling. Be sure hair is completely dry before using styling tools such as a curling iron or straightening iron. You may also be wise to apply a prestyling product whose label reads "heat-protecting." Apply the iron as short a time as possible on each unit of hair. As some have learned, hair can be "fried."

For very *straight* hairstyles, use your blow dryer with a nozzle to give you focused, direct air. For *naturally curly* hair, complete air drying is best. Or use your blower's diffuser attachment. *Fine, thin* hair gets weighted down with heavy styling products. Instead, just apply a light mist of finishing spray. Humid days can make a hairstyle go *frizzy*. Frizz may be defeated by a smoothing spray product. Give your hairstyle *volume* by flipping hair in the opposite direction from its normal growth direction or its usual part point. Don't *overspray* hair to hold a style. Hair should look like hair—not like a helmet.

Sun and swimming notes. Just as you need to protect your skin from sun damage, so too you should protect your hair. There are several ways exposure to sun can cause harm to hair. Ultraviolet rays can affect color pigment. Particularly, color-treated blondes and brunettes can turn brassy. It's therefore a good idea to wear a hat whenever possible.

In terms of protection, your scalp is also susceptible to sunburn both where your hair is parted and along the hairline. So wearing a sun hat offers dual protection. If your scalp does burn, apply some aloe vera gel directly to the burned area at bedtime.

When swimming, remember that chlorine can saturate hair very quickly. You can create a shield by wetting hair and combing a bit of conditioner through it before going into the water. Hair should be rinsed with clean water and carefully detangled after swimming. Chemicals and salt can turn hair brassy or even green.

Chemical treatments. It should be obvious that chemicals—bleach, dye, curling, or straightening products—are hard on hair. You can limit chemical damage by giving your hair a deep-conditioning treatment the night before applying any of those strong chemicals.

Kind thoughts for hair. Keep track of how often you're wrestling with your hair by some of the means discussed in this section. Whenever you can, let your hair rest: back off from using styling products and heated styling instruments for a day or two. Vacations are good for hair just as they are for the rest of your physical self. Keep split ends trimmed off.

Nail Care

Nails are a distinctive skin adjunct God made for our bodies. These hard protectors at the ends of fingers and toes are much more functional than we ordinarily realize. If a nail is ripped or bent back deeply into the quick, or if it's torn off completely, we are instantly (and painfully) convinced that toenails and fingernails are important! Our omniscient heavenly Father installed them as a means of protection and strength for ever-active hands and feet.

Fingernails and toenails also give clues not only about how we're treating (or mistreating) them but also about our general state of health. Many of us have had to deal with brittle, easily breaking fingernails. Those fingernail weaknesses usually come simply as a result of our carelessness. It's not difficult to identify likely culprits: too much time with hands in water, using solvents (as in household cleaning products), harsh nail polish removers, and dry weather (either hot or cold). We can encourage fingernail health by adopting some commonsense measures:

- Wear rubber gloves while doing water- or solvent-related chores.
- Wear cotton gloves while gardening.
- Include your nails each time you moisturize your hands.
- File fingernails in one direction only (from outer edge toward center); a sawing back-and-forth motion can cause nails to split.

- Don't pull or pick at hangnails. Instead, clip them close to the skin, then leave them alone.
- Avoid nail polish removers that contain acetone.
- Be aware that some manicurists are careless about sterilizing their instruments; that failure creates infection risks.

Beyond such ordinary nails-related experiences, however, more serious problems may occur. Several times in the past when I've gone to my doctor with some general physical complaint, part of his response has been to check my fingernails. After reading up on the subject, I've found that he was not just checking on blood circulation; other "read outs" could have indicated various physical conditions:

Vertical ridges, white lines, and tiny white spots. These are natural, and they become more pronounced in aging.

Horizontal furrow across the nail. This is called a "Beau's line." It can be a result of major surgery, heart attack, or some other serious illness. It indicates that the nail's growth has been abruptly slowed.

Nail discoloration. Pale, whitish nails indicate anemia. Bluish nails signal insufficient oxygen in the blood. (The latter may be from heart failure, poisoning, or chronic lung disease.)

Redness, swelling, and pain around the nail. These are symptomatic of bacterial infection, often caused by unsterile manicure tools.

Rounding and expansion at finger's end. This is known as "clubbing." It may be hereditary, but the condition can also indicate heart disease, lung cancer, or inflammatory bowel disease.

Ingrown toenail. This painful condition can be caused by shoes that fit poorly or by nail trimming improperly done.

Thick, yellow nails. These appear mostly on the toes, and the condition signals a fungal infection.

Pitting, spooning, or separation from the nail base. Pits are small indentations, and spooning is the nail curling upward. Any of these symptoms may come from psoriasis, iron-deficiency anemia, or hypothyroidism.

Our response to nail problems should of course focus upon the cause and reflect the seriousness of the condition. For most of us, nail problems

are minor, and improvement will come if we simply think more protectively about our nails and provide for their better care. That might include
brush-on nail strengthening solutions that work either by adding thickness
in layers or by absorption into the nail.

Besides being highly utilitarian and important sources of overall health
information, nails are also ornamental. They give a finished, definitive appearance to fingers and toes.

Nails' cleanliness and grooming are important to both their practical
and ornamental functions. Dirty fingernails can be likened to a caravan of
tractor-trailer trucks transporting germs. Clean, well-cared-for nails protect health and enhance attractiveness—loveliness not of hands alone, but
also of the entire woman.

I once read of a woman whose face missed beauty by a considerable degree; nevertheless she was considered a beauty—because her hands were
flawlessly beautiful in appearance and movement. This woman recognized
her hands as her major asset, and she capitalized upon them by giving
them meticulous care and by wearing outfits whose long sleeves and wrist
trims called attention to her exquisite hands. Conversely, I can think of
women who, despite attractive faces, do not leave the impression of beauty
because of poorly kept hands.

Cleanliness, gloss, and shape characterize well-groomed nails. Their
grooming should include keeping the cuticles pushed back from the nails'
surface.

When your hands have been in clinging or staining materials of any
kind, use a nailbrush in hand washing. Check often to be sure your nails
are clean. Remove the normal, unavoidable accumulation of dirt under
fingernails by careful use of a pointed metal fingernail file.

Healthy nails are naturally glossy. Attractive shine can also be enhanced by oiling and buffing or with clear or natural fingernail polish.

If you use colored nail polish, remember that a Christian woman is
wise to avoid garish, super-dark, or ultra-bright colors. The "in" look
doesn't really matter; our guidelines should be, only and always, the
"within" look—within the bounds of subtlety and restraint. It's also

"handy" to remember that colored nail polish calls attention to your hands: people will notice the size, shape, movements, and so forth more than they ordinarily would. My dear little mother never read a book on grooming and beauty, but she had a keen natural instinct. For instance, I remember that because her hands were short and chubby, she avoided using colored nail polish. As she carefully stroked on her clear polish, she'd chuckle about keeping her hands "invisible." And a final word about polish—*never* wear it chipped: chipped fingernail color screams sloppiness!

Maintain attractive nail shape by keeping the cuticles pushed back from the inner ends and keeping the outer ends smooth and gently rounded. As much as possible, fingernails should be uniform in length. One or two worn long with all the others short (or vice versa) gives an odd, out-of-proportion appearance.

There are two unlovely extremes to avoid in fingernail length: down-to-the-quick stubs and birdlike claws. Stubs usually result from biting the nails. Nail biting or tearing normally begins in childhood, and it thereafter becomes a habit that's hard to break. There are several factors, however, that should discourage nail biting:

- the dirt or germs issue (Take a moment to imagine the places your hands have been in the course of even one hour and the numberless germs that have taken refuge under your nails!)
- the unladylike nature of the habit (Nail-biting says immaturity, nervousness, fear, or lack of self-discipline.)
- the ugly hands it produces

Every now and then we may see someone whose fingernails are ridiculously—and impractically—long. Unfortunately, such unsightly finger "ornaments" have proliferated because of false nails and nail-strengthening products.

Toenails deserve better care than most of us give them. They, too, should be cleaned, shaped, and buffed or polished regularly. Their best length is just to the end of the toe, and relatively straight-cut ends will help avoid the painful problems of ingrown toenails.

Oral Hygiene

Teeth are yet another example of God's wondrous human creation. Each tooth in our head is a living component with nerve and blood. Teeth are arranged in our mouth according to their intended purpose: incisors in front for biting, premolars and molars behind them for grinding. The way upper and lower teeth fit together in closure is precisely engineered; any abnormality can affect facial appearance and become a health factor (for instance, contributing to headaches). The part of a tooth we see rising from our gum line is called its crown. The crown is covered with a coat of enamel. Beneath the enamel is hard material called dentin. And in the center of the dentin is the pulp, which contains the nerve and blood supply for the tooth. Each tooth is firmly anchored by roots going into the jawbone.

Teeth, of course, are our efficient, powerful food grinders. They receive what's put in the mouth and prepare it for the stomach. Our baby teeth are temporary; they're replaced between the ages of six and twelve (wisdom teeth appear later). Our teeth do daily, demanding service. With good care they can live as long as we do. Any dentist will tell you that they're worth the effort to care for them: manufactured replacements aren't nearly so satisfactory in their fit or in their service.

Considering the millions of dollars spent annually in advertising toothpaste and mouthwash, it's a wonder that anyone has to be told of the necessity for good oral hygiene. But it's easy to take our teeth pretty much for granted until problems arise. Is that good stewardship?

Teeth should be brushed and flossed after every meal. Tiny particles of food left in the mouth can cause problems of odor, decay, and gum disease. Moreover, some foods and beverages stain teeth and contribute to plaque buildup. Using an electric toothbrush enhances oral hygiene: the bristles operate in the recommended up-and-down direction, the action of the bristles stimulates the gums, and the built-in timer counteracts hasty cleaning.

The best basis for good oral hygiene is a habit of regular visits to your dentist. He and the dental hygienist provide a strategic defense against tooth problems. Neglected or decayed teeth not only cause pain but also can be the source of hard-to-identify infection seeping into the bloodstream. Long neglected, teeth eventually have to be removed.

Like all the rest of our physical self, our teeth are individualistic, with most of the details genetically determined. That includes their whiteness.

Teeth can also become discolored. One color-changing factor everyone must face is aging. The enamel layer thins, allowing the darker color of the underlying dentin to show through, making the teeth look yellow. Tobacco is a major discoloring agent. There are also certain foods and beverages that have the ability to discolor teeth: coffee, cola, and curries, for example. Some drugs also cause discoloration. And fluoride in excessive quantities while a child's teeth are developing can cause mottled color.

How, then, do we maintain whiteness in our teeth? Dentists warn against excessive or overly vigorous brushing—that can worsen the problem by gradually dissolving the enamel and allowing the darker dentin to show through. A consistent oral hygiene program using a teeth-whitening toothpaste is probably sufficient for most people. And your dentist's deep-clean scaling and polishing treatment removes stains that your own brushing inevitably misses.

Serious discoloration may call for stronger measures. If you have such a problem, you would be wise to consult your dentist. He has the professional means to whiten teeth: techniques include bleaching, light exposure treatments, or application of porcelain veneers. Such treatments will, of course, be expensive. While there are at-home whitening products available in tray, strip, and gel forms, a number of sources advise against using them—hydrogen peroxide, the main cleaning ingredient, can actually cause nerve damage or infection.

Crooked teeth and malocclusion (teeth not meeting properly in closure) can be corrected by orthodontic procedures.

A note of common sense seems appropriate here. For whatever reason, we can become fixated upon some aspect of our appearance and, in trying to make it reach an imagined perfection, waste attention, time, and money. Teeth are a valid example. Smiling models with their precisely aligned, bright white teeth look at us everywhere from magazine covers and billboards. We're aware that our teeth aren't like that. Our one or two slightly-out-of-line teeth may suddenly become the focus of every self-inspection in the mirror—and if we continue along that line of concentration, we can make ourselves so miserable that we either demand and pay for unnecessary dentistry or orthodontics or resent the fact that we can't! How silly. American culture is making us think we must have "perfect" teeth. If teeth really are disfiguring or dysfunctional, they need professional whitening or orthodontics. But if they're only *disliked*, they don't! Whatever happened to the days when teeth gave some individuality and personal character to faces, rather than merely being endless repetitions of suspiciously white, braces-aligned projects? In many cases, American women have needlessly contributed to filling orthodontists' garages with luxury automobiles.

We need to care for our mouths not only because of how they look as we talk and smile but also because of how they may exude odor, as well. There are many contributors to bad breath: carelessness, general ill health, food, and drink. In the latter two categories, there are some outstanding offenders such as onion, garlic, and coffee. Bad breath can also result from a stale mouth—the result of simple time passage since your last brushing. We need always to guard against having poorly cleaned teeth or bad breath because they are *offensive* to those around us. No doubt each of us can think of a time when we were assaulted by someone's halitosis: it's a highly unpleasant experience. You probably know someone whose memory automatically includes the smell of garlic. I do. Do we want to create such memories ourselves?

These modern days really leave us with no excuse for having bad breath. There are myriad breath-sweeteners on the market—mouthwashes, sprays, drops, mints, and so forth. We should each make a habit of using them.

The "and so forth" in the above paragraph never and in no way includes *chewing gum*. The mouth-connected habit that most horrifically destroys ladylike appearance is smoking. But gum chewing vies with it for first place! *Any girl or woman chewing gum in public has chosen to do that which says "hick."*

Now wait—before you toss this book across the room because you like to chew gum, let me assure you that I do too. In fact, when I'm deep into composing a manuscript, gum chewing seems to aid my creative juices. *But no one's there to witness the chomping.*

If you're reluctant to be convinced against gum chewing, undertake a week-long test. Watch girls and women everywhere you go throughout the week. Take special note of those who are chewing gum. How can you miss seeing the instant, effective destruction of *refined appearance*? Gum chewing is not refined; instead, it reflects the pasture—where cows stand chewing their cud.

Some few women, protesting against the banishment of gum, have claimed, "But I don't really *chew*—I just hold the gum in my mouth." Nope. Gum is designed for chewing; while it can be "held" in the back teeth or between gum and cheek for a brief time, if not chewed it disintegrates. And even while it's held chewless, it either makes you keep your teeth partially clamped or produces a tobacco-like hump in your cheek.

Clothing Care

Most of us who are rich in eternal holdings lack in earthly wealth. But a thin purse is no excuse for skimping on cleanliness and neatness in clothing. Some of the best-dressed Christian women I know are *not* those with plenty of money and closets full of clothes. Without exception, though, they are scrupulously neat. One freshly washed or cleaned, perfectly pressed dress is better than ten with stains, odor, and wrinkles! Clothes collect soil very quickly when they're worn—not only from contact with externals but also from contact with the body. You simply can't be too careful, therefore, in insuring that your clothing is clean.

Washable garments should be laundered according to attached fabric instructions *after every wearing.* That certainly includes panties, bras, and other out-of-sight wear. Out-of-sight means closest-to-the-body, with its unavoidable scents and excretions.

For outerwear, be leery of accepting permanent press labels at face value. More often than not, to make such clothing really look its best you must press with a steam iron after the piece comes from the dryer. Don't consider "almost smooth" good enough—after all, it's not the *size* of the wrinkles that count but their *presence*. Wrinkles say carelessness or laziness.

Wool, silk, linen, and some rayon clothing present a different cleanliness problem. Because of the high cost of dry cleaning, it's usually impractical to clean a garment after every wearing. Therefore, such fabrics demand special care during and after wear.

The wisest protection you can provide for any dry-clean-only outfit is to wear underarm shields. You can't count on 100 percent effectiveness from any deodorant, and even a tiny bit of perspiration can cause odor as it permeates the fabric. Certainly, too, a full slip or half slip plus camisole should be worn under the garment, providing a barrier between the body and most of the garment.

Let the outfit hang where air can circulate freely through it for an hour or two after each wearing. *Don't* put the garment back into your closet immediately. After its airing, be sure to make a thorough, careful inspection. Check the entire outfit, giving particularly close attention to the neck, sleeve edges, and underarms. If there is any sign of griminess or odor, send the garment to the cleaners. Your expense is preferable to someone else's *offense*!

Maybe in reading this chapter, you think, "I don't have *time* for all this!" But you do—because scrupulous cleanliness and neatness is more *depth* of attention than *length* of attention. In most cases a girl or woman can simply apply intensified effort in each area of personal grooming. But if you've heretofore skimped in the various aspects discussed in this section, you may indeed have to spend more time on grooming. Consider it an investment toward excellence: excellence of *testimony*.

Or perhaps you react with guilt to the very idea of taking time for careful grooming. Some Christian women have picked up the notion that *all* concern and effort should be spent on others. But, according to God's Word, that's not true. Even the well-known verse "Look not every man on his own things, but every man also on the things of others" implies some concern for self—otherwise, it would read, ". . . but every man *instead* on the things of others." Or consider that wonderful woman of Proverbs 31. There are roughly eighteen verses dealing directly with her various attributes and accomplishments. One of those reveals the obvious care she bestows upon herself:

> *She maketh herself coverings of tapestry; her clothing is silk and purple.*
> **Prov. 31:22**

If we were to translate those eighteen verses into hours (about a normal workday's length for any of us), we could safely say that she spends one hour of her day on herself. Without that self-respecting attention to her own well-being and appearance, she might serve others with a martyr's complex or an embittered spirit—either of which would disqualify her for honor!

Why is good grooming important to a Christian woman? Because it is an outward reflection of the inner reality of her salvation. There are no smudges, tears, or sagging hems on the beautiful garment of salvation as it comes from the hand of the Lord Jesus Christ. Nor does heaven, the eternal home toward which we journey, contain anything but that which is perfect, clean, and bright. Because an eternal God cared enough about the cleanliness of our soul to pay the unutterable price of His only Son's blood, the housing of our immortal souls should surely be the object of our best, our most careful and consistent grooming efforts.

Spiritual X-Rays

> *Take heed to yourselves, that your heart be not deceived, and ye turn aside, and serve other gods, and worship them.*

God's constant focus is upon our inward self—the real self that molds and motivates everything we do outwardly. His most stringent demand is that we be *clean*. In order to be clean in the eyes of the Lord we must submit every area of heart and life to Him. We do that by daily searching the written Word and praying for the enlightenment of the Living Word.

In order to discern between clean and unclean we must present every choice to our heavenly Father with the spirit "not my will, but Yours,

Lord." What we like, enjoy, or judge to be acceptable is not important. What He approves is all-important. A specific case in point: music. You or I may like country and western or rock. That is not the issue. The question, rather, is what that music does to our internal self. Kneeling alone before the Lord, we have to acknowledge that it does not have a positive effect: the moral darkness of the music casts shadows into mind, heart, and soul. Internal darkness inevitably seeps into external involvements, choices, and actions.

This chapter has covered a great deal of ground. But for the born-again Christian, the physical concentration should have a spiritual parallel and balance. While it's certainly legitimate to direct attention to the care and appearance of the mortal physical body, a Christian woman has a broader consideration: the eternal, spiritual body of Christ's blood-bought believers. Each one of us who are members of that body has responsibility to care for it—both as a whole and for its individual members. The apostle Paul not only referred in a general way to the church but also addressed us as its members:

Now ye are the body of Christ, and members in particular. **I Cor. 12:27**

Our concerns for and responsibilities toward the body of believers parallel those for our physical body. The glorious, God-created body of which we are a part is also called the bride of Christ. What wonderful reality! And yet, just as in the case of our intricately woven earthly body, so too of the church—we take it for granted; we neglect its proper, essential care.

Health. The church of Jesus Christ can't be beautiful if she has poor health. Honest evaluation sees signs of weakness and disease everywhere. Are we, as individual members, faithfully guarding against sin's invasion? In the physical body, the most horrendous cancer can begin as one tiny cell gone awry. In the body of the local church, just one member harboring sin can spell ultimate destruction. Rather than bemoaning the faltering condition of the church as a whole, we each need to practice nutritional intake on a daily basis. It's only as the *parts* thrive in good health that the *whole* can do so.

Cleanliness. This is an essential element. The Old Testament book of Ezekiel gives a graphic, dramatic description of love that reaches out to rescue, lift, purchase, and cleanse a sinful, destitute woman. The powerful picture, though, can provide only a faint likeness to the far greater love, lifting, purchase, and rescue Jesus Christ performed on Calvary's cross for wretched, sin-bound humanity. So, then, as those who have experienced that transformation from wretchedness to royalty, do we conscientiously and consistently care for the bride's cleanliness? Do we daily wash our own person in the water of the Word? Do we pray for our local body of believers, earnestly petitioning God's cleansing? Do we exercise discernment in order to detect and combat elements of ungodliness invading the message or the music?

Care of the parts. Think back over the earlier sections of this chapter. We focused upon different portions of the body, considering their importance to the whole and the special care demanded by each. The same principles apply spiritually. By nature each of us would devote our time, attention, and care to ourselves, letting others fend for themselves. But God through the apostle reminds us that we are not just to consider our own individual unit but to demonstrate care for the rest of the body and for each of its other separate parts. Every individual was created to perform and is assigned a place for a particular, necessary function. Each also is interdependent with all others.

> *That there should be no schism in the body; but that the members should have the same care one for another.* **I Cor. 12:25**

Are we occupying our place, content with it? Contentment contributes to vigor; discontent drains energy. Are we functioning faithfully, investing our unique capacity for the good of one and all? Are we encouraging cohesiveness, rejoicing in and enhancing the unity made possible through the blessed Holy Spirit?

The testimony a Christian woman or girl bears through her physical being credits or discredits the Lord Jesus daily here on earth. Her healthy, clean contribution to the church will resound throughout eternity. The two concepts go hand in hand.

Generation Considerations

Teens

Let no man despise thy youth; but be thou an example of the believers, in word, in conversation, in charity, in spirit, in faith, in purity.

While youth is rightly an exciting and enjoyable time, it's also a time that's frightening in its importance because you're making decisions that will affect your entire life. In this building phase, do take great care to choose material that's solid, durable, and increasing in value: things of the spirit. Those choices won't be easy, because young people around you will opt for none of those. Their desire will be toward whatever looks good, feels good, tastes good, and makes them proud: things of the flesh. And they'll want you to keep them company, choosing the same things. But because you're a born-again believer, you must be different as a young person—persistently guarding and strengthening your soul.

Your soul is always to be your first concern. Then, as you keep close check on your internal condition, you can also move ahead to learn proper care for your external self.

Just about everything covered in this chapter on grooming requires two things for success: personal analysis and establishment of solid habits.

Let your mother help you in these two critical areas. She enjoys seeing you transition into womanhood. The walk together as you move over the bridge into maturity can be a special, sweet time of blessing for both mother and daughter.

There might also be an opportunity when girls in your church youth group or Christian school can get together under appropriate leadership to search out the best grooming plan for each of you. Such group sessions can add fun to the process.

Mothers

That our daughters may be as corner stones, polished after the similitude of a palace.

The first phrase in this verse I've chosen to use for the "Mothers" sections throughout the book needs to be addressed here at the beginning—

That our daughters may be as corner stones . . .

What a provocative simile. Cornerstones are typically granite or marble—the type of stones that can have their surface polished to a lovely gloss. Thought of the basic material mentioned here should give every Christian mother pause. How much more clearly could God possibly have indicated the need for strength? That essential is meant to be a guiding force in every aspect of our mothering: a daughter is to have the strength of godly character. Without that, any and all surface polishing will be wasted. Godly character is made up of many things. Among them are

- purity
- wisdom
- temperance (self-control)
- compassion
- diligence
- obedience
- honesty

So as we move ahead into various matters having to do with polish, always keep before you and your daughter that the basic material is strategic. As the polishing process takes place, so too the shape of the stone itself must more and more conform to

Jesus Christ himself being the chief corner stone. **Eph. 2:20b**

Therefore thus saith the Lord God, Behold, I lay in Zion for a foundation a stone, a tried stone, a precious corner stone, a sure foundation **Isa. 28:16**

Do be interested in every aspect of polishing too! It would be a shame for you to miss out on your daughter's transition into womanhood because you're busy doing something else. Though she may not express it (or even seem to appreciate it), a daughter's automatic "primary look" is to her mother. This is a time of great opportunity to establish a unique bond that can grow through all the years that lie ahead.

Mentors

Shewing to the generation to come the praises of the Lord, and his strength, and his wonderful works that he hath done.

Your opportunity is to demonstrate that which is classic Christian womanhood. You can be a living illustration to women and girls coming along after you that good grooming is ageless. The Titus 2 woman best fulfills her responsibility to teach, of course, through her example. I remember with immense gratitude the several older Christian ladies who crossed my life's path and by example encouraged my best efforts in grooming. They inspired the response, "I want to be like that!"

Caution Lights

Take heed therefore that the light which is in thee be not darkness.

While you recognize the importance of and try to practice good nutrition, avoid too-rigid restriction of caloric intake; it's an extreme, and it's dangerous. (Eating disorders are discussed in the next chapter.) And, finally, beware of food or vitamin "evangelists." They—and their claims—represent unbalanced positions to avoid.

Time and effort are of course demanded if you're to be well groomed, but it's also easy to go overboard and waste attention, time, and money. Read and reread the Spiritual X-rays portion of this chapter. Remember, always, that the physical self you're tending is only a mortal, temporal thing. And keep a practical eye open in this regard, as well. For instance, are you hogging the bathroom? A clean, neat self shouldn't take precedence over "clean, neat" consideration for other people.

CHAPTER FOUR

A Lighted Dwelling

CHAPTER FOUR

A Lighted Dwelling

For the commandment is a lamp; and the law is light; and reproofs of instruction are the way of life. **Prov. 6:23**

Following a discussion of basic nutrition and health issues, as in the preceding chapter, it's natural to focus now upon a major component in good health: weight control. Thinking back to the Harvard Medical School's Healthy Eating Pyramid, note that weight control is part of its base.

The topic of body weight comes up frequently in conversations, the communications media touch upon it regularly, and we think about it personally—but too often all of that surface consideration becomes no more, in Shakespeare's words, than "sound and fury—signifying nothing." Something needs to change.

While the Bible sometimes uses "fat" as an indication of blessing, it's not commending physical poundage or being overweight. It's speaking of spiritual richness. There is, however, a highly interesting passage that subtly but tellingly comments on overweight:

And it came to pass, when he [a messenger] made mention of the ark of God [which the Philistines took after killing Eli's sons], that he [Eli the priest] fell from off the seat backward by the side of the gate, and his neck brake, and he died: for he was an old man, and heavy. And he had judged Israel forty years. **I Sam. 4:18**

Eli was not an admirable man. Though he had a spiritual position, he had little spiritual possession. He was insensitive to Hannah's pain of soul, slow to recognize God's call to Samuel, permissive toward his sons' blatant ungodliness, and self-indulgent in consuming the food that made him "heavy." Eli is a Bible character who illustrates how a seemingly minor weakness can be part and indicator of a pervasive character flaw.

When we discuss weight, we're not talking so much about what our skeletal framework does to the scale needle, but more about what our fleshy outline does to it. And what variety there is in fleshy outlines!

The basic determiners of our body weight are (a) foregoing factors: bone structure, body type, and metabolic rate, and (b) ongoing factors: how, what, when, and why we eat.

Genetic bone structure is divided into three categories: small, medium, and large. A tall, large-boned woman should not expect to weigh the same as a tall, small-boned woman. Her bones *alone* weigh more. And because the bones are larger, it takes more "meat" to cover them.

Body type, too, has three divisions: endomorphic, ectomorphic, and mesomorphic. The endomorphic type tends to weightiness while the ectomorphic body is naturally slender, and the mesomorphic build is muscular and athletic. Recognizing the existence and characteristics of these physical types can help you complete your query "Why do I . . . ?" with regard to weight.

And finally, metabolic rate influences weight, that is, the efficiency with which we assimilate and utilize food. In this aspect, too, there is great variation: hence, your highly energetic, thin-as-a-rail sister versus your more sluggish, weight-tending self. Although metabolism is basically genetic, it also both reflects and is affected by eating patterns and exercise.

Modern America sets us up for overeating, and a great many of us fall prey. Statistics show that over 61 percent of adults in the United States are overweight. We're thereby killing ourselves; we're also destroying our healthcare system via weight-related illnesses. Consider the seriousness of just one health threat posed by overweight: heart problems. One study showed that obesity *doubles* the incidence of heart failure in women, and a man with just twenty-two pounds of extra weight stands a *75 percent greater* chance of heart attack than a man within his healthy weight range.

These distressing numbers and their accompanying warnings are readily available. But all the while, the American food industry increasingly tempts us toward gluttony. Figures released by the USDA indicate a 236-calorie-per-person-per-day increase between 1987 and 1995. That caloric intake (which by now has undoubtedly risen) translates into an average 24-pound weight gain per person per year. Yet in 1997 food companies' advertising came behind only auto advertising; they spent $11 billion trying to get us to eat their goodies. Moreover, restaurants keep offering bigger servings, and food becomes available to us at more places.

As Christians we mustn't mimic the world in its blame shifting. It is ridiculous to scream accusations at General Foods or McDonald's. The fault lies in ourselves. We *choose* what and how much we eat.

After consulting many sources, I'm convinced that the best guidelines for weight have been established by the Harvard Medical School. I quote a passage that should have the power to stop any one of us in our tracks and awaken us to the seriousness of being overweight:

Three related aspects of weight—how much you weigh in relation to your height, your waist size, and how much you gain after your early twenties—strongly influence your chances of having or dying from a heart attack, stroke, or other type of cardiovascular disease; of developing high blood pressure, high cholesterol, or diabetes; of being diagnosed with postmenopausal breast cancer or cancer of the endometrium, colon, or kidney; of having arthritis; of being infertile; of developing gallstones; of snoring or suffering from sleep apnea; or of developing adult-onset asthma (*Eat, Drink, and Be Healthy*, p. 35).

Medical experts have established a means of accurately determining anyone's proportionate weight within a healthy range and at what point he or she is overweight. It is called the body mass index, or BMI. It's important for each one of us to know our BMI. You can figure your body mass index by using a mathematical formula:

- your weight in pounds
- divided by your height in inches
- that number divided by your height in inches
- that number multiplied by 703 = your BMI

The resulting number tells it all, categorizing us by means of what we weigh and showing at what point a person becomes overweight:

- 18–25 = healthy weight
- 25–29.9 = overweight
- 30–39.9 = obesity
- 40 and over = morbidly obese

So the guiding principle for weight is this: you should work either to *keep* that strategic number between 18 and 25 or work to *get it down* to that.

Whatever your BMI numbers disclose, note that *effort* is going to be demanded. There are a few people whose weight naturally stays within the healthy 18–25 range throughout life; but they're rare. For the rest of us, maintaining a positive BMI means working to offset the weight-gain factors of overeating, increasing age, decreasing physical activity, and a naturally slowing metabolism. For those who are overweight, there is the more intense battle to lose poundage and bring oneself into the healthy BMI range.

Because so many have problems controlling their weight, because adding pounds subtracts from health, and because being overweight can have an adverse effect upon Christian testimony, some serious thinking—and serious life adjustment—is in order.

No matter how long or how determinedly you may have clutched excuses about being overweight, you need to get rid of them. Medical research shows that even the "glandular problems" often claimed as excuses are almost always overeating, sedentary lifestyle problems.

Gluttony could well be called the ignored or forgotten sin among Bible-believing Christians—but no matter how consistently it may be overlooked from (and in) the pulpit, it is no less a sin! Let's pause for some definitions. A "glutton" is described as "a person who eats or consumes immoderate amounts of food and drink." And "gluttony" appears a bit farther down the page as "excess in eating or drinking" (*American Heritage Dictionary of the English Language*). Note, please, the skewering words "immoderate" and "excess" in those definitions.

Ah, but the dictionary isn't to be the believer's source of convincing; the Bible is. So think how God's Word connects strongly with those definitions.

Let your moderation be known unto all men. The Lord is at hand. **Phil. 4:5**

Hast thou found honey? eat so much as is sufficient for thee, lest thou be filled therewith, and vomit it. **Prov. 25:16**

Further passages such as the following are also applicable:

Be not among winebibbers; among riotous [gluttonous] eaters of flesh: for the drunkard and the glutton shall come to poverty: and drowsiness shall clothe a man with rags. **Prov. 23:20–21**

(Evidently, gluttony should be kept out of our lives even by association!)

God's warnings against self-indulgence do not stop with its effect upon externals—they are issued with an eye to spiritual implications:

And every man that striveth for the mastery is temperate in all things. **I Cor. 9:25**

But I keep under my body, and bring it into subjection. **I Cor. 9:27**

He that hath no rule over his own spirit is like a city that is broken down, and without walls. **Prov. 25:28**

Because overeating manifests weak self-discipline and pandering to fleshly desires, it weakens the testimony God wants us to bear for Him.

Listening to a young woman give her testimony concerning her weight loss of nearly one hundred pounds and her increased usefulness to the Lord thereby, I was particularly impressed to hear her tell how conviction had taken hold of her. Each mealtime she would faithfully bow her head and pray, "Bless this food to my body." That phrase all at once cut to her heart as she realized the incongruity of asking the Lord to bless her sin of gluttony! Standing slim and radiant on the platform, this girl went on to say, "I was *miserable* when I was fat! I was ashamed of my weakness, ashamed of my weight; I hated me. I knew that my fat was a terrible testimony to the elementary school children I taught. I wouldn't go back to that misery for anything!"

Food, of course, is intended as the fuel for our bodies. When our food intake outstrips our physical demands, however, it builds excess fat. And medical studies show that every pound of extra fat works against the body's peak efficiency and health. So, despite all efforts to equivocate, *we put on weight because we put in too much food.*

"But," you may wail, "You don't understand *why* I overeat!" By that, you're referring to some emotional or psychological motivation behind your food-intake problem. You may point to one or more of the following:

- "I'm lonely."
- "My husband isn't what he ought to be."
- "My circumstances are awful."
- "I'm worried."
- "My life is full of insecurities."
- "Nobody loves me."

Coming up with a "reason" is the automatic human response to rebuke or blame, isn't it? In essence, it's an excuse mechanism, an attempt to dodge responsibility and to shift blame. Before dealing with the nebulous "why" of eating, let's look at the more clear-cut, ongoing food-intake characteristics in the order mentioned earlier: how, what, and when we eat.

How do you eat? In the car, dashing between errands? Standing at your kitchen counter? Reading a book? Watching TV? Any of those is thoughtless eating.

What do you eat? A diet heavy with meat, potatoes, and gravy? Fast food? Lots of sugary or highly salted snacks?

And *when* do you eat? Do you skip breakfast? Do you eat at indeterminate times, as you can snatch a moment? Are you always eating? Do you skip meals, then raid the refrigerator at midnight?

Now, we'll come back to the *why* of your eating. I wouldn't discount for a moment the reality and severity of problems like those stated earlier. But wait a minute. Loneliness, marriage problems, tough life circumstances, uncertainties and fears, feeling unloved—all those are matters of the mind and heart. Yet the eating response obviously targets the body. Such a response, then, is a masking or deflecting attempt. *Does stuffing really help?* If you're honest, you'll have to admit that it does not. In fact, it makes matters worse—because unnecessary food consumption and the resulting weight gain add guilt feelings on top of the original problem.

From the practical standpoint, getting a handle (or a brake) on your poor eating habits is best approached from the how, what, and when direction. Each one of those can be changed and controlled. Recognize that conquering overeating demands one tough, tough character trait: *self-discipline.* In fact, control of food intake may call for a greater degree of self-discipline than most other areas of temptation because food consumption is basic to our physical existence.

The manner, or how, of your eating should be changed by making each meal just that: a real meal for which you put aside other concerns and sit down to eat—slowly and deliberately. The "how" should also reflect what I call a "moderation mindset"—ending a meal before you feel full-y satisfied.

The type of foods and the amounts, or what, you consume, too, can be changed, with heavies replaced by lights, avoiding fast foods, and cutting back sharply on sweets and salty foods. A "serving" of a single food or a full course is *not* a heaping mound or an overflowing plate.

The times and timing, or when, of your food intake is also important and should be regulated. The general consensus urges three meals a day with small, light snacks midmorning and midafternoon. It's especially important to eat breakfast. Breaking night's fast is the proper way to awaken one's metabolism for the day. It's also wise to eat your biggest meal at noon rather than in the evening and not to eat again before bedtime. That's because metabolism slows in the evening, preparing the body for sleep.

The emotional aspects, the why, of eating are a much tougher subject. My dear lady friend, it's useless to seek solutions or compensations for emotional needs in food. Instead, the correction of the problems lies in giving your heart burdens to the Lord: *"Casting all your care upon him; for he careth for you"* (I Peter 5:7). "Casting" is a continuing-action verb: we're not just to give a troubling aspect of life to God once, but to do it repeatedly. The greater the problem, the more constant must be the casting. We throw our burdens upon our burden-bearing Lord by talking to Him in prayer and by letting Him talk to us through His Word. But that spiritual consideration is not just a tack-on thought or a disconnected effort. *While* you patiently and persistently present your heart needs to God, you must also patiently and persistently do your part—pushing away from the table. The prayer discipline and the practical discipline will be mutually beneficial, and the sense of helplessness will begin to ease.

So many times when difficulties come into our life, we respond in the flesh. That is, we focus on the circumstance or the person or people involved, and we stew in the boiling emotional pot of helplessness. We *are* helpless to regulate other people or to control circumstances. But we are *not* helpless against our own responses: those are *chosen*—both in terms of our attitudes and our actions. So, in the instance of compensational overeating, a Christian woman must discipline herself against it and bring herself into obedience to Scripture's numberless exhortations regarding self-control.

When you acknowledge the sin of gluttony, and you determine to lose weight for the sake of your health, your self-discipline, and your testimony, can you expect the Lord to make the fat melt? No. You put it on— you're going to have to get it off! The hard fact is, every excess pound we carry can be dropped only via the rigors of exercise, appetite adjustment, and intake control: *dieting.*

Weight-loss diets abound, and each one touts some particular technique or dramatic success. Ultimately, however, weight loss results from just one equation: *less fuel ingested than energy expended.* On paper that makes sense, and it doesn't seem too hard. Taking the equation from paper, though, and translating it into daily reality is another thing entirely. The first three letters of the word "diet" may seem to say it all: you feel that in such self-denial you'll just d-i-e, die. But of course it's not *that* bad. In fact, a sensible weight-loss diet doesn't take you to the verge of starvation. And that should be the first thing you consider in choosing any diet: is it practical for you right now for the take-it-off stage, and is it practical for lifetime adaptation? Essentially that's what has to happen: you must make a *lifelong* change of eating habits. Our family contains a living, breathing example.

There are many things in our daughter, Roxane, that bring delight and pride. One of those is what she has accomplished in weight control. She's had a tough fight. She is only 5'3" tall. She has a physical handicap that severely limits her ability to exercise. She likes heavy, fatty foods. She has an active sweet tooth. She went through more than ten years of constant weight gain, putting on pounds with the birth of each child. By the time she had borne three children, Roxane was carrying a great deal of extra poundage. Then quietly but determinedly she set out to reverse the trend. Only she and our family doctor knew of the campaign. Until, of course, the weight loss began to be evident. At the end of a year, Roxane had dropped sixty-five pounds. Even more important, she has maintained her greatly slimmed self ever since. That maintenance makes continuing demands: she exercises regularly, with those techniques and weight machines she's capable of using. (Though she's a homemaker, mother, and elementary schoolteacher, and she must drive ten minutes to her exercise site.) She also has established an entirely different relationship with food: she, not it, is now in control. Having returned to her college-days figure, our daughter not only looks better but she also feels immeasurably better in every way. Her visible self, most importantly, is now consistent with her God-loving soul; many speak of the challenge she presents to them by her example of self-discipline.

I said earlier that God will not make your excess weight disappear. But He *will* help you. Or do you mentally insert an exception clause in Philippians 4:13?

I can do all things through Christ which strengtheneth me.

Nor should Scripture be used just as a single-plank springboard from which you leap into the weight-loss pond. Bringing temperance—self-control—into your eating patterns really isn't a one-area project. Self-discipline should mark every part of a Christian's being and life. Chances are, your physical tendencies are an echo of your spiritual tendencies: big "meals" on Sundays and haphazard, catch-as-catch-can Scripture "nibbles" the rest of the week. And consider how you've been nibbling—just a sweet bit from Psalms every now and then, missing the vigorous spiritual exercise of Bible study and the healthy balanced diet of the Word's bread, meat, and water. *That* intake and exercise pattern certainly needs to be adjusted! Actually, it should be adjusted *first*.

Job said:

> *Neither have I gone back from the commandment of his lips; I have esteemed the words of his mouth more than my necessary food.* **Job 23:12**

And of course you know God's own commendation of Job:

> *There is none like him in the earth, a perfect and an upright man, one that feareth God, and escheweth evil.* **Job 1:8**

God's Word is as important as our physical food. Why, then, do we keep our souls on a starvation diet? Why do we substitute the "fast food" of easy-read, frothy devotional books for Scripture's perfectly balanced nutrition? Each one of us *daily* needs to go apart unto the Lord, to dig into His Word in order to know Him and to learn of His heart, that we might obey and live to please Him.

See your doctor for a thorough physical examination before starting on any weight-loss diet plan. Confirm the weight you should reach, and have him suggest the severity, length, and type of diet you ought to follow.

Make up your mind that you will succeed on this weight-loss project. As you renew your mind with Scripture, apply that fresh thinking to your weight-loss project:

- Think positively about healthful foods.
- Set short-term, incremental goals, and recognize each one reached as a success.

- Don't allow "martyr" thinking, as in telling yourself you can never again have such-and-such a food.

Such fresh thinking accords with Philippians 4:8, doesn't it? Forget past failed attempts, and lock in mentally for success. Then pray: confess your gluttony as a sin against the Lord Himself and against the tabernacle of His Holy Spirit. Plead His forgiveness and claim His empowering for success. That prayer for strength is going to have to be repeated over and over throughout the days of your dieting, and then on into the years of maintenance.

Unless you join a weight-loss group or professional organization, make the Lord the only one you talk to about your diet. Keep it a matter of covenant between the two of you. The effective dieter is one who doesn't talk about her eating regime—she uses all her energy to stick to it!

Experts agree that decreased eating and increased physical activity must be combined in order to lose weight and to keep it off. We might think of those two factors as conjoined twins. Let's call them "No" and "Go." No keeps us from wrong food choices; Go keeps us exercising. Following are just a few ways to employ the twins.

Employ No

- when your thoughts want to turn to food
- when you feel a slight twinge of hunger
- when the fat-rich, sugary items want to jump into your grocery cart
- in the temptation to weigh daily (Once a week is enough.)
- to second helpings—period
- to "hidden" calories, as in salad dressings; instead, use lemon juice
- when the refrigerator seems to beckon you
- to more than *one bite* of dessert (That's always where the best real taste enjoyment is, anyway!)
- to whatever triggers your urge to snack—TV, reading
- to white-flour carbohydrates
- to a gnawing sweet tooth (Fool your taste buds—eat a lemon or a dill pickle.)

Be satisfied with slow but steady weight loss. "Crash" diets are unwise and unsafe. The first, easiest weight lost by the body is basically just water. But weight that comes off quickly also comes back on quickly. Realize, too, that throughout your reducing program you will occasionally hit "plateaus" where your weight will hold steady for several weeks. *Don't throw the diet out the window!* Stick with it—eventually your body will adjust downward, and you'll begin losing again.

Change your thinking from "get it off" to "keep it off." Roller-coaster weight is not only mentally and emotionally discouraging but it's also harmful to your physical temple. In order to maintain a weight level, most of us have to accept the fact that *for the rest of our lives* we'll have to watch our scales and our dinner plates carefully.

Once you've trimmed down to a healthy weight, a good rule is to limit yourself to a two-pound weight gain. If the needle on the scale indicator swings up to that two-pound limit, cut back immediately on your food intake. Don't be tolerant with yourself! **To win the battle of the bulge, one must be a career soldier.**

Now, here are some ways to use Go:

- for dedication to daily exercise
- for consistency. Experiment to find the time of day and the type and combination of routines that work best for you. *Schedule* exercise time; "If I get to it" doesn't work.
- easy at the start; work up incrementally in your overall exercise intensity and length. Starting "cold" (too fast, too intense) after being sedentary can strain muscles and even cause injury.
- for really demanding exercise. You need to sweat. You need to huff and puff. Your muscles need to burn a bit.
- for sensible warm-up and cool-down periods as "bookends" for each exercise session

Dieting can leave you flabby. Exercise eliminates flab internally as well as externally. Moreover, it's a boon for your cardiovascular system and it works to help curb and redirect your appetite. Don't consider exercise a "maybe" part of your diet but a "must."

Beyond the practical aids prescribed above for weight reduction, the born-again woman can claim Scripture help:

Set a watch, O Lord, before my mouth; keep the door of my lips. Incline not my heart to any evil thing, to practice wicked works with men that work iniquity: and let me not eat of their dainties. **Ps. 141:3–4**

Anyone who has ever tried to lose a pound can tell you that it's no snap! Dieting means hunger pangs, unsatisfied cravings, and an occasional twinge of self-pity when you're sitting next to your best friend while she devours six rolls dripping with butter. But weight loss and control also mean some tremendous pluses for a Christian woman:

plus for your energy and endurance

plus for your character growth through self-discipline

plus for your testimony before unsaved and saved alike

Dieting may seem a very small battlefield in thinking of the great spiritual warfare in which we believers are engaged. Nevertheless, it is a field of encounter with our adversary (it's certainly not the *Lord* who whispers, "Oh, go on—indulge yourself in those unnecessary calories!"); all too often, the encounter becomes a Waterloo. What we learn by enduring hardness in a "little thing" like diet can be used of the Lord to strengthen us for the greater spiritual battlegrounds that lie ahead. And through our Savior's moment-by-moment strengthening we can gain, claim, and keep the land formerly held by self and the flesh.

Eating Disorders

A Christian woman or girl may not only mistreat her body and mar her testimony by being overweight but she can also wreak havoc upon the Spirit's dwelling place via an eating disorder. The two most common of those are bulimia and anorexia. In the briefest terms, bulimia can be described as a pattern of binge-and-purge eating while anorexia is self-starvation.

While there might be a horrified initial reaction to the thought of a Christian having such a serious eating problem, it's best to put aside that response, realizing that a believer is not superhuman in any sense of the word: she's made of flesh, blood, mind, and heart. Just as her body may contract the same diseases that strike unbelievers, so too her internal self may create the twisted pathway to an eating disorder. There is, in fact, an added element of danger within Christian circles due to the heightened desire to hide or deny anorexic or bulimic behavior because it's "unthinkable," or not the mark of a victorious Christian. That means an undiscovered bulimic or anorexic young woman might seriously worsen in our midst, whether it be at home, school, or church.

Both bulimia and anorexia are self-induced behavioral maladies. Both also have roots in societal influences, emotional pressures, and personal thought distortion. Society's contribution comes via glorification of thinness. (Studies show that eating disorders appear almost exclusively in industrialized countries that have adopted Western values.) Emotional pressures may take a number of forms, but change, loss, or lack of control is usually involved. Personal thought distortion takes the form of self-hatred, unreasonable desire for control, or extreme fear of overweight. Both anorexia and bulimia are most often found in adolescents and young adults. Disturbingly, however, experts note a rising number of cases in children. Roughly 90 percent of anorexics and bulimics are female. There is also a high risk for eating disorders among those involved in sports that have weight-related requirements (e.g., gymnastics, track, and cross-country).

Before beginning a description of and warning against anorexia and bulimia, I'd urge you to turn back to page 76, where the Body Mass Index is presented. In particular, take note of the wide range in the numbers that indicate healthy weight: 18 to 25. While they urge us to stay *within* the healthy range, medical professionals do *not* insist that we reach or remain at 18! That lowest number in the range is too thin for many women. Certainly, too, a BMI *below* 18 is cause for concern just as is one over 25.

Anorexia. It usually begins as a weight-loss diet and often follows some stressful change: for example, puberty, parents' divorce, college entrance, a broken engagement. Symptoms include extreme weight loss; intense fear of gaining weight; strong dissatisfaction with body size, shape, or appearance; missing several menstrual periods; hair, skin, and nail problems;

great sensitivity to cold temperatures. Anorexics fall into two categories: anorexia restrictors reduce weight by extreme dieting; anorexia bulimics do so by purging. However it's done, self-starvation is the ultimate accomplishment, and it can result in death.

Bulimia. This disorder is more common than anorexia. It often begins with a diet that fails to result in weight loss. The girl then begins purging in reaction to the failure. Then an eat-and-react cycle sets in: she binges on food, then purges (by forced vomiting or use of laxatives, enemas, or diuretics). The bulimic may also get into heavy use of diet pills. As in anorexia, bulimia, too, has two subtypes: purging bulimics regularly resort to laxatives and so forth, nonpurging bulimics use fasting or excessive exercise after an eating binge. Symptoms include eating an inordinate amount of food in a period of two hours or less; a sense of lost control due to the eating binge; recurring compensatory measures; depression and anxiety; and insomnia and irritability. Bulimia, like anorexia, leaves permanent physiological scars. They include potassium loss, harm to the overall digestive system, erosion of dental enamel, and gum recession.

Even in a non-Christian context, eating disorders are characterized by secrecy, isolation, and shame. In Christian circles, those may be greatly heightened and thus result in extended captivity by the disorder, worsened physiological harm, and ultimately the tragedy of self-destruction.

Let me urge from a burdened heart, in the strongest way possible, for all of us to have an awakened awareness toward eating disorders. If you are a person caught in such a snare, or if you suspect someone you know to be so trapped, *take action!* Seek, please, both spiritual and medical help.

Spiritual X-Rays

Take heed to yourselves, that your heart be not deceived, and ye turn aside, and serve other gods, and worship them.

Examine your first response to this chapter with its concentration on weight control. What was it—anger? Denial? Self-justification? *Why?* Aren't all of those self-serving and self-motivated? Don't they indicate that we feel this physical body belongs to *us*? Doesn't that spirit deny Christ's ownership and the Holy Spirit's occupancy?

The person who eats more than she needs is essentially surrendering her command post, in the spiritual sense; she's allowing her flesh to gain the victory. And of course this mortal flesh is never fully satisfied, is it? It always wants more; one indulgence just makes it yearn for another.

So think about it—intensely and honestly—the next time you bow your head to ask the Lord's blessing on what you're about to eat: is that prayer a mockery? Could there be a spiritual root to the physical weed? For instance, are you under conviction for sin—either because you're unsaved or, as a Christian, holding on to something you know displeases God? Spiritual-physical connections can be highly intricate: you may be trying to smother the "still, small voice" under the heaps of food you're eating.

As our physical concern with regard to weight should be *good health* and *good appearance*, so should our spiritual concern. A soul can grow emaciated if we feed it the "junk food" of feelings and rationalization. Our self-focused mind and our self-coddling emotions drain nutrients from our soul. Conversely, a soul can grow monstrously fat and sluggish from ingesting spiritual food but never exercising. Witnessing, teaching, discipling new converts, rendering physical and spiritual care for Christian sisters—these are the spiritual calisthenics we need in our daily schedule so that we can maintain a healthy, vigorous internal silhouette.

Generation Considerations

Teens

Let no man despise thy youth; but be thou an example of the believers, in word, in conversation, in charity, in spirit, in faith, in purity.

It's important that you don't interpret healthy weight as model-thin. Fashion models are pathetic creatures whose whole life is bound up with a camera lens. The price of such "glamor" is high: ruined health and empty lives.

Mothers

That our daughters may be as corner stones, polished after the similitude of a palace.

The food you give your children from babyhood onward—its quality and its quantity—can set either good or bad patterns for life. *Create a taste in your children early for healthful foods,* and be careful not to fall into the clean-your-plate syndrome or the candy-for-good-behavior trap. Either one can later spell weight battles and health problems for your children.

Mentors

Shewing to the generation to come the praises of the Lord, and his strength, and his wonderful works that he hath done.

Again, you can inspire by example, and simultaneously your controlled weight can lend you energy for a rich life of personal reward and of reaching out to help others.

Caution Lights

Take heed therefore that the light which is in thee be not darkness.

We can get out of balance in emphasis upon the physical. As an example, a family's constant criticism and teasing of one member's overeating can work a result exactly opposite to the one desired. Particularly in the case of a girl, early allusions to her body's size, proportions, and so forth can instill an unhealthy self-focus. I remember one case in particular. The mother of a full-bosomed girl made a major point of reminding her daughter of her bust size and warning her dramatically against any clothing, posture, action, and so forth that might draw masculine attention to her bosom, The result was a girl who developed an unhealthy focus upon physical bodies—both male and female.

In the case of general overweight, teasing and nagging can drive a person to eat even more in an attempt to comfort her wounded heart. The better way is to keep healthful foods and snacks available, set an example of disciplined eating, and pray for her to acknowledge her problem and move to correct it.

CHAPTER FIVE

Closet Lights

CHaPTer FIVe

Closet Lights

Bless the Lord, O my soul. O Lord my God, thou art very great; thou art clothed with honour and majesty. Who coverest thyself with light as with a garment: who stretchest out the heavens like a curtain. **Ps. 104:1–2**

Having dealt with various matters of our physical tabernacle itself, let's now consider what to wear and how to wear it in terms of style, coordination, and appropriateness.

Clothes don't *make* a woman, of course, but they certainly *mark* her. What does your clothing say about you?

It's typical of the feminine nature to be interested in clothing. Nor is interest in clothes condemned by Scripture except as it gets *out of proportion* in our lives. Remember that the virtuous woman of Proverbs 31 is described as being dressed in "silk and purple." In other words, she's *very well dressed*! In her day, silk was the finest, most expensive fabric available, and purple was the rarest of dyes. But let's think further about appearance.

God demonstrated early on with His people that He is interested in clothing. Go back to the book of Exodus, specifically, to chapter 28. You'll see that in giving instruction about His worship He not only mentioned how His priests were to be dressed but He also designed the garments! The effect He intended is not left to our conjecture; He says they were *"for glory and for beauty."* Moreover, when the great I AM communicated to Moses His design for the tabernacle, where He would dwell, He instructed that beautiful, rich colors be used—blue, purple, and scarlet. Pure gold was to be used in its decorations and in its instruments, and the embellishments, whether carved or embroidered, were to be skillfully wrought. The later temple would be even more magnificent.

We Christians are "priests unto God" through Christ's cleansing blood as well as temples in which the Holy Spirit dwells. Thus, we bear responsibility to seek the kind of loveliness in appearance that glorifies God and reflects His beauty.

Perhaps the most extended and powerful Scripture passage that validates a believer's proper concern for clothing is found in Ezekiel 16. God through Ezekiel is berating Jerusalem for her turning away from Him. The passage is dramatic and eloquent: Jerusalem is likened to a forsaken, pitiful, cast-out infant who was without worth and without hope. Yet God rescued her, took her to Himself, gave her a position of honor and a life of richness. Especially interesting for their application to our subject are verses 10–14.

> I clothed thee also with broidered work, and shod thee with badgers' skin, and I girded thee about with fine linen, and I covered thee with silk. I decked thee also with ornaments, and I put bracelets upon thy hands, and a chain on thy neck. And I put a jewel on thy forehead, and earrings in thine ears, and a beautiful crown upon thy head. Thus was thou decked with gold and silver; and thy raiment was of fine linen, and silk, and broidered work: thou didst eat fine flour, and honey, and oil: and thou was exceeding beautiful, and thou didst prosper into a kingdom. And thy renown went forth among the heathen for thy beauty: for it was perfect through my comeliness, which I had put upon thee, saith the Lord God.

Every one of us sinners saved by the glorious grace of God can see ourself in that passage, knowing it to be true of Christ's transformation of our dark, hopeless soul.

Surely by implication, too, we can see that God in no way condemns beautiful clothing or ornamentation. The key for us lies in verse 14; it bears repeating:

And thy renown went forth among the heathen for thy beauty: for it was perfect through my comeliness, which I had put upon thee, saith the Lord God.

The crowning element we each need to aim for with regard to what we wear and how we wear it is the perfecting, beautifying touch of the Lord's own light of beauty shining into and through us.

Secular texts on personal appearance go directly to methods of building an effective wardrobe. Because this text is written to Christians, however, there is spiritual groundwork that must be laid.

Modesty

One concept must be an absolute for a born-again girl or woman: modesty. Yet that clearly presented command from God's Word is increasingly violated as Christianity capitulates to the ungodliness that surrounds us.

God's first act for mankind after the fall into sin was to cover their nakedness. When God later gave the Law, He specifically forbad "uncovering the nakedness." Man and woman's sexually distinctive body areas were to be their "secret parts." God has never changed His mind. The Bible repeatedly stresses that adults (except, of course, within the marriage relationship) are to be clothed modestly.

A Christian's considerations of modesty don't just begin and end with such things as skirt length or clinging fabric. We are to have an entirely different mindset. Besides the core principle of honoring God there is also the responsibility of undertaking for a weaker brother. We need to park here for a bit and bring some practical, honest attention to bear.

We who are female learn early on that those who are male are unlike us. But we are *so very unlike* that there are some things about the masculine composition we may never wholly understand because "we ain't one."

As I look back upon my own youth and as I observe girls and young women today, I firmly believe that much of the problem of immodest clothing among Christians is not deliberate—it's just dumb. Clothing is often worn because it's "in" fashion or because an outfit is cute, or pretty, or sharp. Cute, pretty, or sharp may be light-years away from what a teen-age boy or a man thinks of that outfit. He may think, instead, "sexy." And from that point on he has to do battle against sexual arousal. The male human being's sexual wiring system is unlike the female human being's. It's as if the indicator needle is constantly hovering at ON. In this one regard, then, Christian men may be considered the "weaker brother." We women and girls must not cause them to stumble.

> Let us not therefore judge one another any more: but judge this rather, that no man put a stumblingblock or an occasion to fall in his brother's way.
> **Rom. 14:13**

Sexuality is a special, precious creation of God. For both man and woman, His design was for marvelous heights of intimacy, fulfillment, trust, and joy within the sacred bond of marriage. But the Destroyer, Satan, works tirelessly to blast the design. When you read Scripture carefully, you cannot miss the fact that violating the emotional and physical and spiritual gift of sexuality causes unique destruction.

> But whoso committeth adultery with a woman lacketh understanding: he that doeth it destroyeth his own soul. A wound and dishonour shall he get; and his reproach shall not be wiped away. **Prov. 6:32–33**

The same destruction comes to the woman involved. Intimacy becomes violation; fulfillment changes to frustration; trust turns to suspicion and betrayal; joy evaporates into agony. All that was meant to be beautiful becomes grossly ugly. Body, mind, heart, home, and life become as ashes blowing in the wind.

Ah, but that's not what the world advertises, is it? The public school system begins "liberating" children with twisted sex education in kinder-garten. Then the entertainment media and the advertising industry see to it that human bodies are reduced to the likeness of meat displayed in a butcher shop. We're bombarded with the message that we should live like animals—copulating wherever, whenever, and with whomever we have opportunity. America has come to the place that "sexuality" trans-lates most accurately into "sewer-ality." And it's not only the unsaved who swim in that sewer; Christians do as well. That fact is nothing short of tragic.

Every one of us needs to examine herself minutely to discover and dislodge any particle of "sewer-ality" in our thinking. It takes hold, ladies, without our even realizing it. It affects married women and singles, old and young alike. Married women can get sucked into the sewer with thoughts of their unmet emotional needs, lack of attention, boring household routine, and so forth. Singles may feel a rising desperation due to social pressure or advancing age, making the "anything that wears pants" prospect seem reasonable and to be pursued by whatever means. As for older women, read some recent statistics about American seniors shamelessly living together without benefit of marriage. And young women have been so thoroughly programmed by the media that mental sewerage isn't even recognized. Oh, yes, unclean thinking may have taken root in any of our minds.

God's people must call a halt to our descent into the sexual cesspool. We must come back to God's eternally settled Word and begin *obeying* it in our temporally unsettled world. That is a personal, spiritual transaction in which we submit our mental processes to the Lord Jesus:

> Casting down imaginations, and every high thing that exalteth itself against the knowledge of God, and bringing into captivity every thought to the obedience of Christ. **II Cor. 10:5**

Obedience of Christ casts out sewer thinking and replaces it with thought processes that meet the high standards found in Philippians 4:8—*true, honest, just, pure, lovely, of good report.*

Christ-directed thinking will recognize sexuality as a precious, beautiful gift to be protected and preserved—whether for just one person within marriage or for no mortal but as part of our fidelity to God.

Christ-obedient thinking will acknowledge purity to be an essential for every area of life—and particularly for our sexual life.

A Christ-loving mind will eliminate fashion dictates and hold firmly to modesty requisites.

The Bible tells us plainly that as believers our life purpose is to glorify God. With regard to modesty, then, a born-again woman or girl must ask a basic question each time she dresses: *"Does this outfit honor God?"*

Because American Christians are so constantly and blithely violating modesty principles, I'm going to write in plain and specific terms.

What are our "secret parts"? For a woman that means her breasts and her bottom (pubic area, buttocks, and genitalia). What are the marks of immodesty? There are many characteristics of everyday clothing that can in fact or in effect uncover our secret parts:

- low necklines (Any neckline that exposes the beginning swell of the breasts or the beginning of cleavage between the breasts is decidedly too low.)
- gapping necklines (These are simply sloppy when you're standing up straight but revealing when you have to bend over.)
- panty lines
- cropped tops that show skin at the midsection
- gapping armholes (These allow a view of the breasts from the side.)
- transparent tops
- low-cut slacks or skirts
- tight tops (They expose the breasts by defining them. There should be at least one inch of fullness in fabric at the bust line.)
- knit fabric, as in T-shirt material that not only defines the breasts but also reveals the nipples.
- white or light-colored skirts that become transparent when the sun or another strong source of light shines through them
- tight skirts, culottes, and slacks that hug the pubic area or cup under the buttocks. (There should be at least one inch of excess fullness at the hips' broadest point.)
- clinging fabric that reveals body details or bra or panty lines
- skirts with slits that go higher than the knee
- culottes or pants that cut up between the buttocks
- above-the-knee skirts (They make modest sitting impossible.)

When I think of above-the-knee skirts, my mind goes back to a comic first line in a rhyme parody of Joyce Kilmer's poem "Trees"—

I think that I shall never see

A thing as ugly as a knee.

The parody continues in like manner. It certainly makes a valid point although the real issue is the modesty violation.

Some of the things just mentioned may seem unnecessarily restrictive. But this is a matter in which *masculine makeup* must be taken into account. In making mankind male and female, God saw fit to create the male with sexual instincts that are aroused by what he *sees,* while the female responds most strongly to *touch.* Saved or unsaved, men are alike in this basic, instinctive sexual aspect; the difference lies in their *reaction* to the stimulation of sight. The ungodly man seeks, revels in, and succumbs to it. The godly man, on the contrary, must curb and confine it. Our responsibility, therefore, as Christian women, is great: we must NOT dress in such a way as to promiscuously stimulate boys and men.

Modesty serves not only as a protector of our physical purity: it simultaneously protects our vital core of being. Sexuality is less a part of what we do than of what we *are.* Any woman who has been sexually abused or raped will tell you that her *soul* was bruised by that violation. Sexual purity is a treasure to the one who preserves it and a precious, unique gift for the one to whom it is ultimately yielded in marriage.

Neatness

God is a God of order. All of His creation is marked by exactitude. Neatness is a characteristic or expression of order. Trends toward a "dress-down" and a comfort mindset have quickly translated into sloppiness. Everywhere you look, you see tackiness. Americans' ragtag appearance proclaims its source: self-centeredness. Wear-anything folks might as well carry a sign that says, "Whatever I like, I'll do." "Whatever's easy, I'll wear." "I don't care what anyone else might think or how they might respond to my looks." Dare we Christian women wear such proclamations?

How can they possibly be made to fit with the Bible's multiple urgings toward awareness of and concern for others?

Your clothing's neatness during wear depends, first of all, upon accurate fit. Seams should rest exactly in their intended places—not half an inch east west, north, or south. Waistline and shoulder seams are the greatest offenders in this regard; but vertical seams, too, can be askew. Whether you purchase or make your clothes, insist on precise fit. A narrow-shouldered woman wearing a dress with shoulder seams hanging halfway to her elbows can't hope for a neat appearance. Neither can a long-waisted woman look neat if the waistline of her dress rides her midriff. Both these examples are exaggerated to highlight the importance of accurate "lay" in seams. *Poor fits are misfits.*

Unless you are the one-in-a-million woman whose frame fits the mythical sizing scale, you'll rarely find ready-made clothing that is *really* ready—for you. Most of us have to deal with one or more places in a garment where measurements don't fit ours. Whether shopping or sewing, impatience may whisper, "Nearly right is good enough!" But if we're going to look our best for the Lord, we must consistently resist the whispered urging. Misfits not only detract from appearance; they also detract from the wearer's attitude because they're uncomfortable. Therefore, a few clothes that fit perfectly are worth closets full of misfits.

Principles of Fit

There are guidelines for knowing whether a garment fits. It pays to look for them in each item of clothing you try on. Poorly fitting clothes don't look neat.

Jackets
- Collar and cuff roll lines lie flat with no gapping.
- Jacket shoulder is ¼ to ½ inch wider than blouse shoulder.
- Sleeve reaches wrist bone and allows ¼ to ½ inch of blouse sleeve to show (Coat sleeves should be ½ inch longer than jacket sleeves.)

Dresses/skirts

- Waistline falls *at* your natural waistline (unless, of course it's intended to be dropped or empire).
- Skirt waistband allows room for two fingers to be inserted.
- Straight skirt has at least one inch of excess fabric at fullest point of your hips.
- Pleats and vents lie flat, not pulling or spreading.

Blouses

- Neckline hugs base of neck—no gapping or wrinkling.
- Sleeve shoulder seam hits at your pivot bone.
- Bust darts point to and stop one inch from bust point.
- Front doesn't pull tight or gap.
- The tail has adequate length to stay tucked in.

Slacks

- Waistband allows two-finger room.
- Side-seam pockets lie flat.
- Pleats lie flat.
- Two or three inches of excess fabric are at hips' widest point.
- Creases fall straight.
- Crotch length is comfortable and modest.
- Hemline touches top of shoe.

When you're checking the fit of a garment, don't just stand still and check yourself in the mirror. Move: bend, sit, reach up over your head.

Another destroyer of neatness is a garment's poor construction. Examine every piece of clothing carefully before you buy. Look for the following signs of shoddy manufacture.

Seams

- fewer than ten to twelve sewing stitches per inch
- skimpy seam allowance (less than ⅝ inch)
- *pucker*

Collar

- not lying flat; bulky at edges, points, or corners
- pucker at notches and/or corners

Zipper

- thread that doesn't match fabric
- stitching crooked or puckered
- zipper teeth exposed

Stripes/plaid

- patterns mismatched at seams
- uneven pattern at the hemline

Top stitching

- thread mismatched with fabric (unless it's intended as contrast trim)
- crooked or uneven stitching

Hem

- ridge of stitching shows from right side of garment
- puckering or sagging

Buttonholes

- stitching too widely spaced (fabric can ravel)
- loose threads

Buttons

- poorly attached to the garment
- loose threads
- no accommodation by thread shanks on bulky fabrics

Bras and slips can destroy neat appearance in several sneaky ways:

- a slip hanging longer than the hem of the outerwear
- a slip too short for a garment (Correct length is just to the top of the outfit's hemline.)
- a half-slip "crawling" and lumping because of static cling
- a slip or bra strap falling off the shoulder
- a half-slip worn under a semitransparent garment (*Always* wear a full slip or half-slip plus camisole under such clothing. No matter how lightly the unsaved world may treat the display of undergarments, Christians cannot do so without violating modesty principles.)

- a belt pulled too tight (to compensate for a misfit in waist size?). It makes the outfit look like a sausage tied in the middle.

There are other neatness killers as well.

- rundown shoes
- reinforced-toe hosiery with open-toe shoes
- knee-high hosiery worn under anything shorter than ankle-length-with-no-slit
- hose with runs
- dandruff or lint
- missed buttons or other "left undones"
- lining hanging out
- hands-in-pockets habit with skirt or slacks that pulls the fabric into awkward lines or reveals panty lines
- too-short coat over a longer skirt
- pilled fabric

Determine to become your own neatness policewoman: always double-check your entire self front and back in a full-length mirror before you step out the door.

Femininity

It is vital to remember that "male and female created he them." The unsaved are dedicated to erasing or distorting the differences God created—but that "unisex" effort must be shunned by us who know the Lord through personal, saving faith.

Mannishness probably invades women's wear most effectively in denim pants: jeans. Produced under a multitude of labels, bearing huge variations in their price tags, and with their fabric put through all sorts of "distinctive" torture treatments, jeans are everywhere. They are *too much* everywhere.

Denim pants are wonderful at appropriate times—horseback riding, working the field or barn, hiking, spring skiing, and so forth, but to wear them constantly as they are by American women and girls is ridiculous.

In the first place, most jeans defy the modesty principle because of tightness. But there's another negative effect; they exert a subtle but pervasive influence toward masculine carriage. Women sitting spraddle-legged or with ankle-on-the-knee leg crossing has become increasingly evident as jeans are increasingly worn. As another perhaps minor but telling observation, there's the small child moving along the street, in a store, or through an airport terminal behind two jeans-and-tennis-shoes-clad people. Which one is Mommy?

I very much like what my husband says of womanhood: it's "dust twice-refined." He of course refers to God's creation of Adam from dust and Eve from Adam's flesh. How wonderful if we born-again women would consistently demonstrate our distinctive creation!

Webster uses such words as "gentleness," "delicacy," and "modesty" to denote femininity; that which is feminine has a softness and warmth about it. In clothing, that does *not* mean we have to wear ruffles and bows. It does mean, however, that we should consistently strive for "softening" in line or detailing and shun harshness or mannishness. For example, you do well to choose tailored suits for business wear; but avoid carrying the tailored look into the realm of *severity*.

In a nutshell, we Christian women, while avoiding both immodesty and "sexiness," should express our delight in our God-given femininity by our appearance, attitude, and actions.

Practical Wardrobe Guidelines

Underneath it all. A garment's fit, neatness, and modesty are all affected by what is worn under it. Out of sight should not be out of mind with regard to underclothes. Be picky about them, with special attention paid to the support factor. Not just any bra fits any figure, and there are fabrics, sizes, and design details in nearly endless variations. Try on different models until you find the one that's exactly right for you: comfortable but correctly supporting your breasts. Panties should be snug but not tight; otherwise, any extra flesh will bulge over the elasticized edges, creating unsightly panty lines under your clothing. Panties with very high-cut legs are better for eliminating panty lines than are those with regular legs. Bikini panties, however, are particularly bad for creating panty lines at their top.

Support is not just critical for your top but for your bottom, as well. *If you have any shape in your hips and buttocks at all,* you need to wear support—either control-top pantyhose or a girdle. This is a matter at which slobbism is at its very worst in America: for the sake of comfort women are opting out of supportive undergarments, and the result visually is nothing short of awful. Jiggles, bounces, flops, dimples, bulges, and panty lines are abominable showmen.

There are relatively few people to whom you'll be able to speak a testimony for the Lord. There are unnumbered others, however, who are "reading" your testimony daily. They do so via first impressions, and first impressions are almost entirely visual. Studies show that in just fifteen seconds a person encountering you for the first time forms more than a dozen opinions about you and your life. *Does your appearance count as a plus for Jesus Christ?*

A born-again woman or girl should not try to keep pace with the extreme swings in fashion that appear from season to season and year to year. They are a calculated effort of the garment industry to keep the buyer's pocket empty and the industry's coffers full. Yet women by the millions fall for the phony build-ups of "what's new" or "what's in"—a sad waste of energy, emphasis, and money. Secular writers, too, proclaim the foolishness of dressing according to designer dictates. Fashion has reached the point that very few women really look good in the industry's trendsetters. I, for one, resent designers who evidently hate women and manufacturers who play us for financial idiots! Instead of succumbing to the pressures and blandishments of the ever-changing fashion scene, each of us needs to exercise wisdom and restraint—by identifying our own personal style and adapting positive elements of fashion to it.

A good wardrobe reflects a woman's personality, lifestyle, coloring, and physique.

Personality

There are many different personality types in terms of idiosyncrasy details. At the same time, however, there are a few broader categories into which they can all fit. They are called by different names in accordance with how they'll apply. Because we're considering what we wear, I've chosen the terms *casual, charming, colorful, classic,* and *creative* to describe clothing personality types. Your wardrobe should have distinctive markings consistent with your personality. You've probably experienced the "it's not me" response when trying on an outfit in a store or trying a friend's garment that looks so good on her. Each of us feels and looks best in styles and colors that are in sync with our personality. Read through the brief descriptions below. Where do you best fit?

She whose personality is *casual* exudes a warm spirit and an underlying zest for life. She's the girl-next-door type.

The *charming* woman is quietly confident and very feminine. There is an innate softness reflected even in her voice.

The *colorful* lady is often large in frame. She's outspoken and assertive. Others would describe her as striking. Even in casual dress she has a dramatic flair.

She who is a *classic* type has a calm, restrained air. She likes neatness and precision. There is elegance in her bearing and manner.

The *creative* type has a sense of excitement about her. Her thoughts have originality. She may often swing through various levels of emotion. Her idiosyncrasies are evident.

Are you having a tough time categorizing yourself? Ask a friend to help you. Think of women you know who seem to fit the different types. Which is the nearest like you? Ask yourself which type of clothing and setting as described by the terms most appeals to you, and in which you'd feel most comfortable.

Having carefully thought through the categories and decided where you fit, look at your closet contents. Do they positively proclaim your personality?

Lifestyle

Analyze your needs according to the following aspects of your life:

- region
- locale
- focus of endeavor
- social activities

Let's discuss those influencing factors.

Region. The section of the nation in which you live should have a bearing upon the way you dress. Basic climate varies from region to region, making a wardrobe suitable to the Northeast unsuitable to the Southwest. Likewise, the formality of life varies: the East is generally more formal in its clothing than is the West. The woman who wears spike heels, silk dresses, and big floppy hats in an area where sensible shoes, tailored daywear, and bare heads are the order of life calls undue attention (and resentment) to herself.

Locale. Is it urban, suburban, or rural? Clothing worn in a farming community is likely to reflect comfort and practicality while that worn in a large city leans toward sleekness and sophistication.

Focus of endeavor. Upon what does your life center? School? Home care and child rearing? A business or professional career? Differences in life emphasis create differences in wardrobe needs.

Social activities. Their range and frequency of activities will play a part in your clothing choice. In other words, if you often attend luncheons, teas, and receptions, the dressier end of your closet needs to be more extensive than if your social activities consist of weekly church attendance and a yearly family reunion.

Coloring

A key component in a successful wardrobe is color. An expensive, beautiful outfit may look awful on you because it's not in the right color family to enhance your own coloring.

Colors basically divide into "cool" and "warm." Your coloring is a combination of hair, skin, and eyes. But how does the color consideration work? Colors that are right for you have the effect of infusing your own coloring; they make you sparkle. Wrong colors, instead, drain away your coloring; they subtract life from your face.

Take the time to determine your coloring. Have a friend or family member who has an artistic eye assist you. There are three sets of contrast test colors. With no makeup on, and in natural light, stand in front of a mirror that's big enough to show your upper body. One by one, hold large swaths of cloth so that they cover your bust and shoulders and come close to your face. You may need to do each pair several times before you're able to see the differences in the effects upon your face.

White	or	Cream
Black	or	Navy
Silver	or	Gold

If your skin, hair, and eyes take on life from the first column of colors, your coloring is "cool." If instead you sparkle when draped in colors from the second column, you're "warm."

There is a second consideration related to color usage in clothing: intensity. A strong (or bright) color, though in your proper color family, may overpower you. Or one that's pale may make you look ghostly. The key, again, lies in your own coloring: there are vivid blondes and pale blondes; there are vivid brunettes and mild brunettes; there are fiery redheads and Titan redheads. The stronger the coloring of hair, skin, and eyes, the greater intensity of color the person can wear.

Consult a color wheel. Become acquainted with both warm and cool colors. Cools have a blue base; warms a yellow base. Even more important, *learn* from the wheel which colors and what intensities you should have in your closet. There is also another bit of help the color wheel can give you: coordination clues. As you look at one of "your" colors, check the one directly opposite on the wheel: that's a *complement* color. It "goes with" the first one. When combined with the original, it will add life. Colors that appear directly beside each other on the color wheel are "related" colors, and thus can also be used together effectively. And the colors that are to each side of the complementary color are good to use as accents for your original color.

Physique

Finally, consider your physical structure. Never buy or make a piece of clothing because it looks good on a plastic dummy. Most of us are neither undernourished fashion models nor the fabled 36–24–36. To dress as if we are will make us look ludicrous. Whatever our physique, we can dress cosmetically so that our God-given body looks its very best for His honor.

When analyzing body shapes, there are several basic outlines; each torso is one of the following:

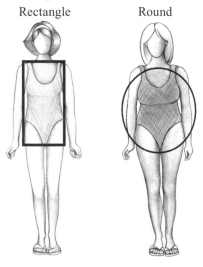

Rectangle   Round

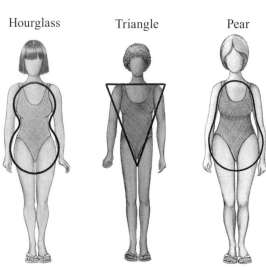

Hourglass   Triangle   Pear

None of the shapes is bad. Each can be dressed attractively. "Cosmetic" or "camouflage" dressing is done by applying principles of proportion, line, color, and texture.

Cosmetic efforts are applied not only to the body outline but also to the body's proportions. Artistically speaking, ideal female physical proportions look like this:

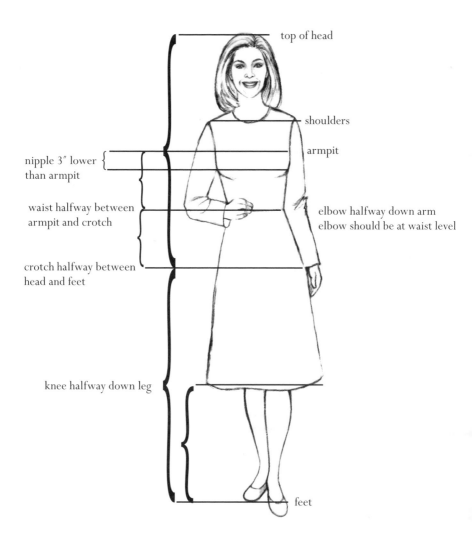

top of head

shoulders

armpit

nipple 3″ lower than armpit

waist halfway between armpit and crotch

elbow halfway down arm
elbow should be at waist level

crotch halfway between head and feet

knee halfway down leg

feet

Variations from the specified proportions give us terms such as "short-waisted," and so forth.

The body's individual structure also takes its character from height and bone size (according to wrist measurement). Those categories are determined as follows:

Height	Bone Structure (wrist size)
5'3" and under = petite	5½" or less = fine bones
5'3"–5'6" = average	5½"–6½" = medium bones
Over 5'6" = tall	Over 6½" = large bones

Camouflage works by deceiving the eye as to relative sizes, lengths, and widths. Its components are line, color, and texture.

Cosmetic use of line (garments have two kinds of line—external and internal) directs, deflects, or deceives the eye of an observer, correcting unattractive reality. For instance, a very tall woman would appear shorter by wearing some horizontal lines (e.g., a jacket with a yoke line above her bust and the jacket hem ending at midhip).

Color is also a wonderful cosmetic device in clothing, and it's one of the simplest to remember: lights and brights attract attention, advance, and enlarge; darks divert attention, recede, and diminish. Obviously, then, whatever area of the body is overlarge should be clothed in darker colors; small areas in lights or brights.

The final camouflage tool is texture. Fabric textures vary greatly, and each type, with its particular characteristics of drape, crispness, and bulk, can be used to visual advantage. For example, an underweight woman would appear more robust in a suit made of nubby tweed than in one of silk shantung.

Specific suggestions for using each of the camouflage tools will be given later.

Building a Wardrobe

Before you begin to do any new building in terms of your closet contents, analyze what's there now. Set aside half a day. Go through your wardrobe piece by piece, judging the following:

- Is it modest?
- Is it me in personality?
- Is it feminine?
- Is it suited to my lifestyle?
- Does it enhance my physique?
- Does it enliven my coloring?
- Is it good in terms of coordinating with other pieces of clothing?

You'll probably find you've created three categories:

- It has to go now. Donate it to charity.
- It can work temporarily while I adjust and revamp my wardrobe.
- It's great. Thank the Lord!

Do not be loath to see your closet contents thinned. It's a step toward simplifying and streamlining. Chances are, you'll discover you really didn't wear the discarded things much anyway.

Every project, to be successful, needs to have a goal. The clothing goal at which each of us should aim is *a wardrobe that says personalized excellence because we serve the God of glory.*

That does not mean numberless outfits. It does not mean spending a fortune. It does not mean devoting great amounts of time, energy, and concentration on clothing. In practical terms, it means having the least number of garments for the greatest number of combinations, with everything modest, appropriate, and enhancing the individuality God has created in us.

Although many, many pages could be (and have been) written on the subject, I'm going to condense to the essentials of wardrobe building.

THE BLUEPRINT: the goal of personal excellence

THE SKELETON: line and color considerations

Line. There are visual characteristics of line that can prove helpful when deciding which garments will do the most to enhance your physique.

Horizontals

- widen (But horizontals high or low on an outfit can slenderize.)
- draw attention
- decrease length/height

Verticals

- elongate
- decrease width

Diagonals

- generally flatter
- the closer to vertical, the more slenderizing
- plaids on the bias become diagonals

Curves

- gentle
- feminine
- those going upward lengthen
- those going downward shorten

Color

The mainstays of a good wardrobe consist of neutrals: basic colors around which everything else works. While the list of core colors has expanded since the 1980s, the principle of unifying through color continues. The idea is to build in compartments of color, each one working around a core color.

If you have a cool color personality, the neutrals from which to choose as core are black, gray, white, dark navy, taupe, burgundy, forest, and cherry red.

As a warm color personality, the neutrals that present themselves are brown, rust, cream, camel, teal, bright navy, olive, and tomato red.

THE LAYOUT: color compartments

In choosing your first color compartment core, realize that the darker the color, the more practical it is. That, no doubt, is why earlier texts on beauty recommended just black for cool coloring and navy for warm. It's still wise to think in terms of practicality and adaptability as you begin updating your wardrobe. The more basic your chosen core for your first compartment, the farther that compartment can extend—and your clothing self-education with it. Dark neutrals are not memorable—which means they can be worn repeatedly without it seeming so. Also, they're appropriate for more occasions.

So your compartment's core color has been chosen. Every piece in or added to that compartment is to coordinate with the core. As you might imagine, separates are easier to work with in coordinating than are dresses. Begin with one color compartment for each area of your life. Each compartment should contain three or four coordinating colors in a number of pieces that can be worn in different combinations. The most effective compartment is one in which each piece of clothing works with at least three others.

There are some principles for coordinating an outfit that are particularly easy:

- all neutrals
- neutrals with one accent piece
- a monochromatic outfit (light and dark of one color)
- a print or plaid plus one of the colors within it

Another bit of safety insurance for bringing colors together in an outfit is to use no more than three: one in greatest quantity, then the second, and the third used just as an accent.

There are also some general placement principles for color in clothing:

- Lighter, brighter tones usually should be at the top of an outfit for visual balance and to draw attention to your face. (The triangle figure, with its greater size at the top, should limit the light/bright just to the neckline as an accent for the face.)
- Avoid stark contrasts in places where you're broad or where it divides the body into two distinct sections.

If you live in an area where the weather extremes don't prevent trans-seasonals, they are your best wardrobe investment. Trans-seasonal fabrics include light wool gabardine, light wool flannel, wool crepe, wool georgette, wool or rayon challis, rayon blend gabardine and crepe, fine wale corduroy, wool or silk jersey, cotton and cotton-blend knits.

Verbal explanations of the color compartment technique can get long, complicated, and confusing. Since a picture is worth a thousand words, here is a sketch of a color compartment.

CORE COLOR: Navy   COORDINATING COLORS: tan and green

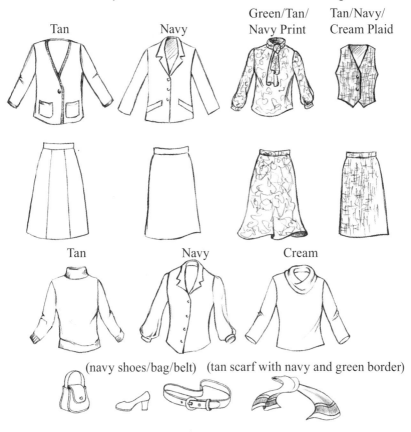

| Tan | Navy | Green/Tan/ Navy Print | Tan/Navy/ Cream Plaid |

| Tan | Navy | Cream |

(navy shoes/bag/belt)   (tan scarf with navy and green border)

Visualize the possibilities in switching the pieces around. They are many—and much easier and effective than trying to coordinate with items bought or made with no thought of unity. Even greater variety can be achieved by wearing the tops as tunics, either belted or unbelted. When you want to expand the compartment, you can pull the green or cream that appears in the print, and get these garments in either color: jacket, skirt, and blouse.

Every piece of clothing should be chosen not only with an eye to color but also with the purpose of enhancing your physique. In this regard, you need to consider the *lines* of a garment. The most concise way to present the principles of line is in list form. Each figure characteristic will be followed by suggestions for flattering and camouflaging clothing techniques.

General Torso Shapes

RECTANGLE	*Use*	*Refuse*
	Pressed-down or inverted pleats	Straight styles
	Soft gathers at the waist	Tight-fitting styles
	If thin, add bulk—texture, color, pattern	
ROUND	*Use*	*Refuse*
	Shoulder and neck emphases	Bulk in texture
	Unstructured or straight jackets	Too much fabric drapery
	Longer jackets	
	Overblouses	
	Diagonal lines	
	Drop waistline	
HOURGLASS	*Use*	*Refuse*
	Rounded lapels	Crisp pleats
	Shawl collars	Stripes and plaids
	Crossover or drape neckline	Set-in sleeves
	Gathered or raglan sleeves	Straight darts
	Soft florals and abstract prints	Restricted waistline
TRIANGLE	*Use*	*Refuse*
	Shoulder pads	Full-gathered skirts
	Pleated or puffed sleeves	Slim tops
	Layering on top	
	Boat, drape, or crossover necklines	
PEAR	*Use*	*Refuse*
	Bulk, color, texture on bottom	Shoulder details
	A-line skirts	
	Soft, fuller skirts	

Heights

PETITE	*Use*	*Refuse*
	Vertical lines	Horizontal lines
	Small-scale prints/plaids	Bulky, overpowering fabrics
	Monochromatics	Oversize trims and accessories
TALL	*Use*	*Refuse*
	Horizontal lines	Vertical lines
	Larger-scale prints/plaids	Small patterns/accessories
	Fuller, softer outlines	Body-hugging outlines

Specific Features

BROAD
SHOULDERS *Use*

Dolman or raglan sleeves	*Refuse*
	Shoulder pads
V-necks	Detailing at shoulder
Long necklaces	Bateau neckline
Horizontal lines at shoulder	

NARROW SHOULDERS *Reverse the above.*

LONG NECK *Use*

High collars	*Refuse*
	Open necks
Neck scarves	Bare neckline
Choker necklaces	Long chain necklaces

SHORT NECK *Reverse the above.*

LONG ARMS *Use*

Long sleeves with wide cuffs	*Refuse*
	¾ length sleeves
Fullness in sleeve	Tight sleeves

SHORT ARMS *Reverse, plus avoid multiple bracelets.*

LARGE
BOSOM *Use*

Shoulder pads	*Refuse*
	High collars
Open and V-necks	Detailing or trims on bodice
Fullness, draping of fabric	Bulky sweaters
(but not loose baggy)	Tightly cinched waists
Short sleeves and jackets	
Overblouses	

SMALL BOSOM *Reverse, plus avoid tight tops; layers and loose fit are flattering.*

LONG WAIST *Use*

Bolero, ⅞ and ⁹⁄₁₀ jackets	*Refuse*
	¾ length jackets/overblouses
Wide belts (in skirt color)	Drop waists
if waist is small	Belts in color of the top
Empire waistline	

SHORT WAIST *Reverse, plus use verticals and diagonals above waist; stand-up collars.*

WIDE HIPS *Use*

Shoulder details and trim	*Refuse*
	Tops that end at the hips
Center seam skirts	Gathered waists; full-pleated
Layering on top	skirts
Either short or longer jackets	Detailing or design at hips

BIG
STOMACH *Use*

Big tops that cover but don't cling	*Refuse*
	Belts
Bulk at waist	

BIG
DERRIERE   *Use*   *Refuse*
           Jackets that hang straight ending   Tight or clinging skirts
           just at top of buttocks
HEAVY LEGS *Use*   *Refuse*
           Longer skirts to just above ankle   Light or colored hose
           Hose matched to shoes, or dark tones   Flat or strappy shoes
SKINNY LEGS *Reverse the above.*

Perhaps in reading through the preceding lists looking for clothing tricks, you came across some unfamiliar terms. Clothing of our modern era has design elements and features that appear repeatedly. Shopping can be smoothed by knowing the name of some element or feature.

NECKLINES

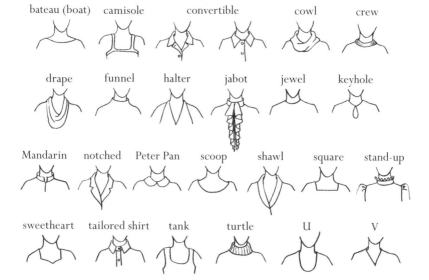

SLEEVES

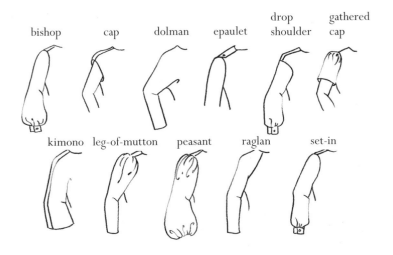

bishop cap dolman epaulet drop shoulder gathered cap

kimono leg-of-mutton peasant raglan set-in

BLOUSES

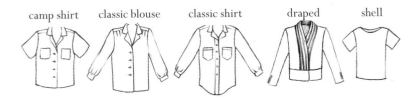

camp shirt classic blouse classic shirt draped shell

KNIT SHIRTS

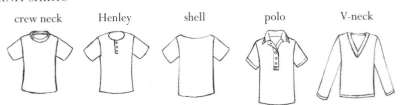

crew neck Henley shell polo V-neck

SWEATERS

cardigan   crew   cowl   V-neck

turtleneck   twinset

VESTS

bolero   classic

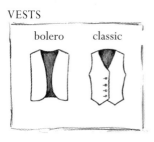

SKIRTS

A-line   contour waist   design pleat   dirndl

flared   pleated   sarong   straight

tiered   wrap   yoke

JACKETS

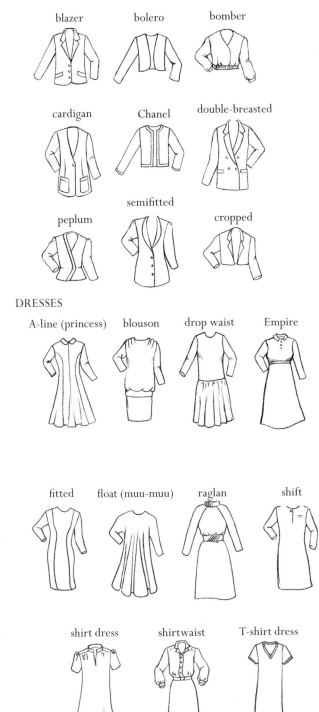

blazer   bolero   bomber

cardigan   Chanel   double-breasted

semifitted

peplum   cropped

DRESSES

A-line (princess)   blouson   drop waist   Empire

fitted   float (muu-muu)   raglan   shift

shirt dress   shirtwaist   T-shirt dress

Accessories

Besides the garments that make up any color compartment, there should be coordinating accessories: a pair of shoes, a purse, and a 1″ to 1½″ belt in the core color, hose in a color that goes with everything, and a scarf that contains and pulls together all the colors.

Shoes, while considered accessories, are also important in themselves. It was interesting to find that even the most recently published sources urged common sense in shoes. There is strong opinion expressed against both super-high heels and clunky shoes. Podiatrists and orthopedic surgeons point out that a heel over 2¼″ high shifts five times your body weight onto the ball of the foot, and a 3″ heel creates seven times more stress on the forefoot than does a 1″ heel. Besides inevitable discomfort, high heels with pointed toes lead to foot problems: ingrown toenails, corns, bunions, pinched nerves, claw toes, and stress fractures. Nor are feet alone in their suffering; high heels increase the risk of knee osteoarthritis.

Then there are the clunky shoes: those types with monstrously thick soles that periodically become fashionable. The black mark against them is sheer awkwardness—not only in appearance but also in their total defeat of the wearer's gracefulness. At the time of this writing clunky shoes are "in" again, and as a result, physical grace is definitely "out."

White shoes are not recommended except for nurses and others whose uniform requires them; white calls attention to your feet, and it's almost impossible to keep clean and neat.

Shoes should be the best and most comfortable you can afford, in leather if at all possible. Once purchased, they need to be carefully maintained—no rundown heels, scuffs, or lack of polish.

Other accessories like jewelry, scarves, and belts should be used, keeping in mind the restrictive phrase "less is more." Particularly guard against too much jewelry. Just because you happen to own ten rings does *not* mean they're to be worn at the same time. And a special note about your most special rings: wedding and engagement rings are properly worn with the wedding ring inside—closest to your heart. The engagement ring is considered a guard.

I was particularly pleased to find that even after twenty years, scarves still win top honors as accessories. Personally, I think they're unbeatable. They take hardly any room in a suitcase, they're easy to use and can "make" an outfit instantly. Not only does adding a scarf draw attention to your face and add interest to a garment, just changing the way the scarf is tied creates a new look.

Finishing Touches

Even for your most casual moments, opt for clothing that doesn't proclaim shallow living and follow-the-crowd mentality. Specific things to avoid include designer names in print, paint, tag, or embroidery.

Aim for *quality* and *simplicity* as you add coordinating colors and pieces to your closet. Together, they will stretch your dollar and your clothing's usefulness.

Hold tightly to the tenet that you get what you pay for! It's important to school yourself in recognizing quality—not just in makers' names but also in construction and fabric details. Make some trips to a fine dress shop or designer area in a department store. You're going there only to gain knowledge—not to buy anything. Examine the clothes for various characteristics that signify quality. Learn the look, the construction, and the feel. Thereafter, always opt for the very best quality you can afford. One quality garment is worth four "make-dos."

Your self-education in quality can be a tremendous asset in all shopping. Although you refuse to pay retail prices, wise buying can get you top-quality clothing. Quality material and construction plus conservative styling in a garment give it long life and happy usefulness.

While most females over the age of three know and get excited about sales, many need to be warned against their danger: impulse buying. A right price does not make an item the right purchase.

The "tone" of an outfit should be consistent throughout—that is, casual and dressy items should not be mixed.

There are three basic terms with which to be familiar in order to dress appropriately: tailored, casual, and dressy.

Tailored clothing has a crisp, businesslike appearance. It is characterized by generally straight, simple lines and conservative, "background" feel in fabrics and in colors such as gray, brown, camel, and navy.

- Blouses—pointed or rounded collars; jabot-tied self-scarf; slim-cut, shirt look.
- Jackets—medium length; lines skimming, not hugging the body; shoulder seams fall at shoulder line, not "dropped." No excess trims. Buttons and belting of same color and fabric. Blazers.
- Skirts—straight or A-line (gathering at waist adds softness and dressiness to appearance).
- Dresses—conservative "background" colors; generally self-trimmed. Straight or A-line skirts. Simple, clean-lined bodice design.
- Shoes—medium heel height; unadorned plain pump in basic or "background" colors.
- Bags—medium size; basic or "background" colors; neat appearance.

Casual apparel gives a "country living" feel to your appearance. Silhouette allows for freedom of movement.

- Fabrics—synthetic blends; cottons; novelty weaves and textures; wools in bulky, nubby, and "cuddly" textures.
- Colors and patterns—bold, bright, light.
- Blouses—drop-shoulder; sleeveless; bowed ties. (Sweaters are almost always casual.)
- Skirts—gathered, gored, full, or wrap.
- Dresses—necks of varying shapes (round, square, Peter Pan); sleeveless, three-quarter, or long.
- Trim—contrast and highlight by fabrics and color.
- Shoes—colored; leather sandals; canvas; cork heels; stacked heels; fat heels; wedge heels.
- Bags—large; accent colors; straw; novelty.

Dressy attire conveys the special-occasion feel. There are various levels of formality within the general category, covering a "church dressy" to "banquet dressy."

- Fabrics—silk, crepe; and drapables. Taffeta, velvet, satin, *peau de soie,* and so forth are generally considered *evening only* fabrics, as are those with metallic threads.
- Colors—deeps, darks. (It's sometimes helpful to borrow from the masculine rule of thumb: the more formal the occasion, the darker the outfit should be.)
- Silhouette—drapings, flounces, shawl collars.
- Blouses—shiny fabrics; metallic threads (these first two are evening only); lace trims; ruffles.
- Skirts—range from very full to very slim; draped.
- Dresses—bateau or cowl prominent among necklines.
- Shoes—patent and very shiny leathers; silk, faille, gold or silver (latter two are *evening only*); slender, high heels; slender-strapped heeled sandals; fancy buckle or bow trim.
- Bags—small; clutch or envelope type; patent leather; beaded or with jeweled ornamentation.

The frustrating thing about categorizing is that it's impossible to cover everything. Within each general type, too, there are different degrees of application; but I've tried to make a listing of item and characteristics most *frequently true* to their own category.

There are a couple of items that need to be remembered for all categories of dress. First, hosiery should be worn with all but the *most casual* clothing. *Bare legs are never appropriate with tailored or dressy things.* And, second, shoes should always be as dark or darker than an outfit at the hem.

For those special occasions when you're given a corsage, be sure you wear it the correct way: with the flowers in the position in which they naturally grow. In other words, the ribbon portion of the corsage will be *below* the flowers.

The woman who represents the Lord Jesus Christ has a responsibility to look her appropriate best at all times. Wise, careful building and use of a wardrobe can greatly aid that worthy goal.

Your Appropriate Best

Building a wardrobe really is wasted effort if the clothing in your closet isn't worn with consistent concern for appropriateness.

Again, the unsaved are trying to jettison all thoughts of appropriate dress: jeans go everywhere. They may go—but they do so against guidelines of acceptability. It is disturbing to see Christians leaning toward that same heedlessness. Dressing appropriately not only indicates culture and common sense but it also boosts your spirit and accomplishment. Various studies bear out that fact. For example, students who dress neatly do better in their class work and earn higher grades than their sloppy classmates. The same is true in on-the-job professional settings.

It doesn't take great wisdom to discern the difference between occasions. It does take in-your-face, I'll-do-as-I-very-well-please to disregard those differences. Nowhere in the Bible can you find such attitudes accepted or commended by God.

Although it shouldn't be necessary to put them on paper—especially for Christian women and girls—here are some basic distinctions:

- The barn and the fields, hiking, horseback riding, skiing, river rafting, and participation in other active sports call for tough, practical clothing such as denim.
- School is a place for neat, clean, and feminine dress—as in skirts, blouses, and sweaters.
- Church calls for a higher degree of thoughtfulness and care in dress: that which is the ultimate in femininity and understated beauty.
- Offices are the place for the seriousness of tailored suits and dresses.

- Operas and classic dramas, fine restaurants, formal dinners and events demand very dressy or formal wear—satin, lace, and so forth.

In case you missed an essential element in that listing, I'll put it down in black and white: *denim does not go everywhere.*

Furthermore, one item particularly in the listing needs examination and emphasis: church. Church for a blood-cleansed individual should be a special and wonderful place. Why? Because we go there *to worship the Lord* in a formal, prescribed setting shared by others of like precious faith. How can anyone who knows God as He is presented in the Bible go to worship Him in an attitude and outfit worthy only of a ballgame or picnic? The "I'll wear whatever" spirit proclaims the feeling that church attendance is something done on one's own terms; God should be grateful that a bit of time is taken for Him.

Sorry. The pervasive attitude just described cannot be justified scripturally. Our mighty, sovereign, creator God *Himself* decrees what is acceptable in worship. Study it out from Genesis to Revelation. There are prescribed conditions for coming before the Lord. When Jesus Christ became man, He in no way erased the necessities for acceptance by God the Father: He fulfilled them. Whereas the Old Testament priest came to worship with fear in his heart and special garb upon his body, we as New Testament believer-priests should also come to worship with reverential fear in our heart and special garb upon our body. God has not changed. We have—and the change is not only abominable; it's frightening. God will not endlessly restrain His wrath against those who claim His name yet degrade it.

Shopping

An effective wardrobe demands wise shopping, and shopping wisdom has some important components.

- Pray. Talk to the Lord about what you need, about your time and money limitations. Seek His help and direction for the entire enterprise.

- Know what you need. Make it a habit to keep a list in your wallet for the sake of that occasional "happy accident" that may appear unexpectedly.

- Shop according to a plan. Organize your trip logically. For example, shop the store that's farthest away first and work toward home; or go to the most expensive first, then work into the discount and resale shops—or vice versa.

- Do your shopping alone. Combining visiting and business makes neither effective.

- Dress well. Wear an outfit that will take you comfortably into the most exclusive stores and departments. Be sure to wear good foundational garments that will make you look your best in everything you try on.

- Shop on a day you have plenty of energy. Menstrual cramps aren't conducive to clear thinking and calculated decisions.

- Eat before you go or stop while you shop. Studies prove that a hungry shopper is an impulsive buyer.

- When you're shopping for a color-match item, take a sample of the original. Don't trust your color memory. Even navy has amazing variations.

- Give yourself plenty of time to find what you need. Hurried choices are usually wrong.

- Shop in the middle of the week. Fewer people will be competing for the items, and clerks will be less harried.

- When trying on an outfit, don't trust a single-view dressing room mirror. Be sure to check everything in a three-way mirror.

- If you're shopping for smaller items—e.g., knit tops, blouses, and so forth—and you find something just right, consider buying multiples. Two of one color provides a useful backup, and a second color expands your outfit's usefulness.

- Whether you're considering quality, color, or fit, don't be satisfied with "nearly right."

While consistently shopping to avoid retail prices, don't think cheap. Instead, hold firmly to the demand for the best quality at the least expense. The ultimate price of "cheap" is almost always high. In this regard, exert special restraint when shopping outlet stores: their markdowns really aren't all that good, and their merchandise is often made up of irregulars or seconds.

I have two friends who represent the ultimate in beautiful, tasteful dressing: Becky and Kitty. Watching and admiring them for years, I've never ceased to be amazed at what might be called their "closet confessions." Invariably when complimented on an outfit, either will respond with a twinkle in her eye as she tells its source: a resale shop. Like them, I've found resale shopping to offer the ultimate opportunity for excellent quality at bargain prices. Garments that apparently were in some rich woman's closet for only one season have thereafter proven to be staples in mine for twenty to thirty years.

Although it was mentioned in the opening portion of this chapter, it bears repeating: *a good wardrobe does not demand great spending in either time or money.* In fact, as the principles are applied and self-discipline exerted, there actually will be great savings in every way. Added to those savings will be incalculable enhancement of your closet contents in terms of modesty, personality, appropriateness, flexibility, and longevity—all of which will strengthen your life testimony for Jesus Christ.

Spiritual X-Rays

Take heed to yourselves, that your heart be not deceived, and ye turn aside, and serve other gods, and worship them.

Let's first focus the x-ray upon our mind. If this chapter leaves you with a mental shrug and the thought, "It's no big deal how I dress," x-ray probing reveals a shameful disregard for your testimony. If you follow through with that mindset, you will thereby validate an unsaved observer's fondly held impression of a born-again Christian:

- sloppy in dress
- stringy, unwashed hair

- colorless, gloomy face
- uncultured
- uneducated
- grimy hands and dirty fingernails
- body odor and bad breath

He or she has created and maintains that picture willingly—as an excuse against listening to the Bible's pronouncements. Time after time it comes out in a testimony of salvation that the first bit of interest in and openness toward the gospel was kindled when he or she met a Christian who contradicted that mental picture. What spiritual responsibility you and I bear for our physical reflection of Christ!

Now we'll focus the x-ray in a more general sense.

No matter how fine or appropriate our closet here, it will ultimately be dust. The clothing items for our soul, however, will be with us throughout eternity. Do we pay constant, meticulous attention to our soul's wardrobe?

Dig into your Bible, looking specifically for passages that tell us

- what to *put on*
- what to *take off* or *put away*
- how to *stay clean*
- differences in *value*

There is one point, in particular, at which concern for and attention to our physical closet can spell deficiency in our spiritual one: pride. When and if designer names, price tags, or store logos become important, we're in trouble.

Generation Considerations

Teens

Let no man despise thy youth; but be thou an example of the believers, in word, in conversation, in charity, in spirit, in faith, in purity.

Clothing is an area in which young people can feel tremendous peer pressure, and being accepted by the "in" crowd can depend upon brand names or garment cut. Learn early that such thinking is sheerest nonsense. Those who subscribe to that scheme of things are extremely shallow and not worth your desire to be with or like them.

Mothers

That our daughters may be as corner stones, polished after the similitude of a palace.

Beginning in her tiny days, keep genuine value before the eyes of your daughter. Point out unlovely attitudes—not only in other people's daughters but in yours as well. For instance, I remember how my mother could instantly bring me down to earth about an outfit by speaking a familiar phrase: "Pretty is as pretty does."

Another powerful leveler is the practice of cutting out labels from garments as soon as they come home from the store, seeing that your daughter doesn't wear brand-emblazoned clothing, and even urging your school to adopt uniforms.

Take great care in the way you monitor your daughter's modesty and purity instruction. Emphasize the beauty and blessing of her sexuality as it's to be reserved for her husband. Too many Christian young women bring a misconception out of their home training: they've been made to think of the whole realm of sex as dirty and disgusting.

Mentors

Shewing to the generation to come the praises of the Lord, and his strength, and his wonderful works that he hath done.

Your silent teaching by example and your spoken commendation for those whose appearance is modest, feminine, appropriate, and lovely can serve as a wonderful standard. Much of my inspiration with regard to personal appearance came from women a generation ahead of me. Their garments of salvation were made visible by their garments of selection.

Caution Lights

Take heed therefore that the light which is in thee be not darkness.

The outstanding danger with regard to clothing is extremism in one or both of two areas: modesty and femininity.

Modesty. Beware of distortion on this subject. While girls and women do of course bear responsibility to avoid causing a brother to stumble, the *ultimate* responsibility is upon the boy or man himself. A male human being is so structured that he automatically looks with appreciation and enjoyment upon a female human being. But after that first look, his gaze is something he *chooses*—in its direction, its duration, and its interpretation. We girls and women do *not* need to dress in clothing that resembles feed sacks or that harks back to Bloomer Girl days. Those are extremes that put a blemish on our testimony.

Femininity. Trouble and inconsistency in this regard stem mainly from unreasonable use of the word "never," and in applying the word with extrascriptural glue to certain pieces of clothing. Femininity choices must take into account common sense and appropriateness. **Skirts and dresses should be our preferred garb in daily public living, and we should delight in their statement of femininity.** However, Scripture does not say "thou shalt not wear pants or slacks" where it forbids women wearing men's clothing and vice versa. When God gave that command, both men and women wore *skirts.* When you look at the Deuteronomy 22 passage so often used, you will see that verse 5 cannot stand alone. It is nestled among many other prohibitions; are any or all of those also claimed for modern application? And, moreover, it was Jehovah Himself who designed "breeches" *for the sake of modesty* in His priests' service at the altar. Men and women in that day dressed much alike; distinctive features were in small things—e.g., embroidery on women's clothing. The principle as seen in its proper context and extending to its modern application would merely prohibit, for instance, women wearing neckties or baseball caps.

Why is it that Christians become rigid, unbalanced, and self-righteous in exactly the places where God balances responsibilities and allows flexibility?

In the opening of this chapter, I mentioned that we must maintain proportion in our womanly interest in clothing. We will keep our priorities straight if we consistently keep our eyes and emphasis upon the clothing of our souls. Meditate much upon the blessed passage in Isaiah that reads,

> *I will greatly rejoice in the Lord, my soul shall be joyful in my God; for he hath clothed me with the garments of salvation, he hath covered me with the robe of righteousness, as a bridegroom decketh himself with ornaments, and as a bride adorneth herself with her jewels.* **Isa. 61:10**

CHAPTER SIX

Mirror Illumination

CHaPTer SIX

Mirror Illumination

Truly the light is sweet, and a pleasant thing it is for the eyes to behold the sun. **Eccles. 11:7**

Now we come to focus upon that fascinating, roughly oval expanse of tissue and tones, bony planes and fleshy hollows by which the Lord has depicted our identity, character, and personality: our face.

Have you ever noticed in Genesis how God chose to describe Rebekah?

And the damsel was very fair to look upon, a virgin. **Gen. 24:16**

Those two phrases tell of her countenance and her character; her prettiness and her purity; her loveliness and her life. As the Lord looks at you and me, can His heart similarly join the two dimensions? Anytime we expend effort and time on externals, we should simultaneously check up on our internals, as well: is there so complete a joining, so compatible a likeness the one to the other in us as in Rebekah?

For a woman, added to the importance of personal identity is the built-in desire for comeliness. That desire, when properly channeled and controlled, is legitimate. Can anyone honestly imagine that God's very first, handcrafted woman, Eve, was anything but supremely lovely? The continuing yearning for personal beauty was placed within our nature by God Himself. The *abuse* or *misuse* of that yearning certainly does dishonor

Him. But how can we sensibly contend that the Altogether Lovely One is honored by a feminine face that's deliberately or ignorantly unlovely?

I was highly interested to find in several sources reference to the fact that the *inside* woman ultimately determines the beauty of the outside woman. Those sources were secular; our Christian viewpoint expands and underscores that concept.

What is your real attitude toward your face? Study your countenance in the mirror. Have you *contentedly accepted* it—good points and not-so-good—as being the one the Lord wanted you to have? If not, you're sinning against the Lord—for you are dissatisfied with the way He made you.

> *Woe unto him that striveth with his Maker! Let the potsherd strive with the potsherds of the earth. Shall the clay say to him that fashioneth it,What makest thou? or thy work, He hath no hands?* **Isa. 45:9**

Or, conversely, are you sinning against God by being proud of the way you look? Pride disfigures the soul and thereby debases facial beauty. Nor does it even make sense for any one of us to get puffed up over something that came as a gift of the Lord.

> *For who maketh thee to differ from another? and what hast thou that thou didst not receive? now if thou didst receive it, why dost thou glory, as if thou hadst not received it?* **I Cor. 4:7**

If you struggle with either dissatisfaction or pride, go apart unto the Lord before you go on in this chapter. In that quiet, heart-to-heart place, verbalize exactly where and how your spirit is disfigured. (God knows it already, and it displeases Him and harms your relationship with Him.) In *genuine* regret for your sinful attitude, repent of it, ask God's forgiveness, and seek His help for maintaining a proper heart regard for His creation of your face.

Once you have come to contented acceptance of your countenance, you can determine to do your best to have the right kind of facial attractiveness. "Attractiveness" must have a special dimension of meaning for a born-again girl or woman. It goes far beyond prettiness. Prettiness is a thing merely of the physical, and it may please the eyes of mankind.

Beauty has its source in character, and it speaks to the soul. In Sonnet 54, William Shakespeare wrote,

O! how much more doth beauty beauteous seem

By that sweet ornament which truth doth give!

And in his play *The Two Gentlemen of Verona* he has a character say,

"Is she kind as she is fair? For beauty lives with kindness."

It is of course Scripture that ultimately defines Christian beauty: *"the beauty of holiness."* That phrase provides the key to our motivation, direction, and limitation in seeking to present our face at its very best.

In thinking toward presenting our face at its best, we come to a question whose answer covers the whole spectrum of personal opinions and preferences: *what about cosmetics?*

First of all, let's establish the definition of "cosmetics." In the 1938 Federal Food, Drug, and Cosmetic Act, they're defined as "articles intended to be rubbed, poured, sprinkled, or sprayed on, introduced into, or otherwise applied to the human body or any part thereof for cleansing, beautifying, promoting attractiveness, or altering the appearance."

Some who staunchly hold the "No artifice!" position are actually pretty inconsistent—they condemn color applied to the cheeks but gladly adopt false teeth; they decry lip color but routinely wear shoulder pads or cologne. Do they *really* mean we should live in the human raw? Wouldn't that demand that we go without deodorants, and . . .

Undue emphasis upon externals is just as wrong on the minus side as it is on the plus side. *Of course* a Christian woman does wrong to paint and posture like a streetwalker. But the one who proclaims "paleness is purity" is likewise off base. There is no redemptive power in a pale face and knee-length hair! Consider, for example, the individuals, sects, and groups whose plain-dress appearance provides only a pathetic camouflage for gross immorality.

In the final analysis, the use or nonuse of cosmetics by a Christian must be dictated by her parents while she's a minor, by her own personal convictions in adulthood, or by her husband's wishes.

In beginning to address areas of personal preference and conflicting measurements of right and wrong, I feel that it's necessary to warn against a major ugliness that is marring some segments of Christian life, testimony, and ministry in our day: self-righteousness.

There are many things about which the Bible speaks clearly either for or against. There are many other areas in which there is no "thus saith the Lord." The latter are areas in which we are allowed freedom of choice. The problem is, where there's no "thus saith the Lord," many want to insert "thus say I." And where that insertion comes, there comes phariseeism, imposing extrascriptural demands upon others. Personal choice, personal conviction, personal preference should be just and only that—personal. None of us as an individual has the right to impose our choice upon someone else. Too, our choice does not make someone else's choice wrong. The minute you and I look down our spiritual nose at another believer who differs from us in her choices, convictions, or preferences, we've turned on the motor of pride, and we're entering the highway of self-righteousness. We can travel the highway in either of two directions, ladies: toward "Well, how worldly!" or toward "Ugh, how plain!"

The apostle Paul lays out this whole thing of personal spiritual responsibility in such a clear way that we're brought to the proper perspective. Chapter 4 of I Corinthians opens with an urging toward faithful stewardship. Then Paul goes on:

> But with me it is a very small thing that I should be judged of you, or of man's judgment: yea, I judge not mine own self. For I know nothing by myself; yet am I not hereby justified: but he that judgeth me is the Lord. Therefore judge nothing before the time, until the Lord come, who both will bring to light the hidden things of darkness, and will make manifest the counsels of the hearts: and then shall every man have praise of God. **I Cor. 4:3–5**

Each one of us who has a personal relationship with God stands daily before Him on the carpet of personal responsibility. It's a single square of carpet—no one can share it. Our heavenly Father's all-seeing eye notes and judges our every thought, emotion, motivation, word, intention, and action. We're to live on that carpet square aware of and obediently re-

sponsive to the fact that our right or wrong is fully *in the sight of the Lord*—
a phrase that appears repeatedly throughout the Word. It is His approval
we're to seek; it's His heart we're to delight; it's His will we're to search
out and to obey.

In many ways, our "small" life choices are more critical than the big
ones. By that, I mean that though we of course obey God's distinct commands, such as "thou shalt not commit adultery," many choices as in matters of personal appearance are left up to us. That doesn't just turn us
loose by any means. Instead, at such points the subtler aspects of our heart
toward the Lord come into action. Obeying the commands and statutes is
one thing; choosing to do right in an undefined area is another thing entirely.

So, friend, keep your eyes on your own square of carpet: it's more than
enough for you to be responsible for!

*For we must all appear before the judgment seat of Christ; that every one may
receive the things done in his body, according to that he hath done, whether it
be good or bad.* **II Cor. 5:10**

In light of this sobering reminder, make your every decision about cosmetics with care and with prayer.

If you decide that you'll not wear makeup, be sure to give your facial
skin careful daily attention so that your appearance is glowing.

Teenagers, I'd urge you not to wear makeup until you have to! Youth
has unique natural color and beauty. Enjoy the ease of getting ready in the
morning that your youth affords you! And how very quickly those young
colors fade on most of us. So comes the time when our face needs a boost.

My family has three distinct types with regard to need for and use of
makeup. My oldest sister is a brunette. Her dark hair and eyes, perfectly
shaped mouth, and vivid coloring have enabled her to be a lipstick-only
makeup person well into her sixties. Even now, in her gray-haired seven-
ties, the only thing she has needed to add is a bit of rouge. My other sister
is a medium blonde with long eyelashes, gray eyes, and olive skin. Her
makeup kit contains only lipstick and mascara: voila—sparkling color
and distinct features. Ah, yes, and then—me. I smilingly say that color

and conformation sort of weakened by the time they passed on down the bloodline to the youngest Peters daughter. My towhead blonde of little-girl days has done a long, slow fade into dark dishwater. My blue eyes are deep set, with one larger than the other, and their short lashes are pale. My lips are over-generous and crookedly shaped. Guess who has a full battery of cosmetic enhancers? I give this personal example to illustrate the vastness of physical differences in faces and why some may need and can benefit from cosmetics.

My husband's grandfather had a country-boy phrase he'd use to state the crux of the matter: "If the barn needs painting, paint it!" But of course "paint" isn't really an accurate word to use when referring to a Christian woman's face because *for the believer, makeup must be a subtle enhancer only.*

If you don't wear makeup, skip what follows. But because I see many Christian women who change "makeup" to "mess-up," I'm going to give a detailed gleaning of information and recommendations.

Skin

Foundation

Even flawless skin can well use the protection a good makeup base affords against the elements. Skin with texture or color blemishes definitely needs it for the sake of refined appearance or smoothed color. Your foundation should be as near your own skin tone as possible. If you prefer, you may instead use a tinted moisturizer.

Don't choose foundation according to its appearance in the container. Test it on your clean skin. Though you're aiming for color enhancement, beware of going too light or too dark. Too-light base will look chalky or gray and will exaggerate imperfections in the skin. Too-dark base will look muddy or dirty. Your best color choice is one that most nearly "disappears" into your own skin tone. The aim should not be to hide your skin but to enhance it.

A note about using foundation as you age. Beware of going darker in the attempt to replace your fading natural color. The effect is hardening. Instead, go toward a lighter tone.

If there are areas on your face that you do want to hide, such as dark under-eye places, apply a concealer before your foundation. Use a concealer that's one or two shades lighter than your foundation. I've personally found that green concealer works best on my skin. But it wouldn't do for all skin tones. Don't put concealer on the entire half-circle under your eyes but only on the portion close to your nose. Dab it on and pat it just enough to set—let the foundation do the blending as it's applied over the concealer. If your dark circles are particularly evident, you may also need to dab on more concealer after applying foundation. Then blend again by pressing foundation very lightly with a sponge over the concealer. Be careful not to put light concealer on any puffiness under your eyes: it will highlight the area. (Remember the color principle that light attracts or enlarges.)

Choose your type of foundation according to your skin's characteristics and needs. Dry skin responds best to creams or creamy liquids. Normal skin does well with water-based or powder-based formulas. Oily skin needs powder-based foundation or oil-free liquid.

Foundation can be applied either with fingertips or a cosmetic sponge. Begin by dotting foundation on forehead, cheeks, nose, and chin. For a light, smooth application of cream or liquid base dampen the sponge before using. If heavier coverage is needed, the sponge should be dry. With a powder foundation, though, a dry sponge delivers sheer coverage, and a dampened one gives greater coverage. Remember to be gentle with your skin as you apply foundation, and use upward motion as much as possible.

Usage notes: Always aim for the least heavy application of foundation; otherwise, it looks caked on the skin and it accentuates wrinkles. Some sources recommend covering lips with foundation, while others say it dries the lips. Be sure foundation edges—at hairline and jaw line—are carefully blended; there should be no line of demarcation. Do not extend foundation down onto your neck—it will just rub off on clothing.

Face Powder

This comes in two forms: loose or pressed. Both accomplish the same thing, so the choice is just a matter of your personal preference. Or you may choose loose powder for home use and the compact type for your purse. (Foundation can begin to look shiny as the day goes along and need a dusting of powder.) Powder should match foundation color. Apply powder to your entire face, then remove excess with a cosmetic brush. Powder softens the foundation's appearance, dulls its shine, and sets its finish.

Usage note: Don't over-powder; the excess accumulates in facial creases.

Cheek Color

This may be called rouge, blush, or blusher, and it comes in a variety of forms: cream, powder, powder-to-cream, gel, and liquid. Your choice will be based upon how well it works on your type skin, plus how easily and effectively you can apply it. Choose a color that is as natural and close to your own coloring as possible. Consider, too, unity of color: you wouldn't wear pink-toned blush with red or orange lipstick tones. In applying cheek color, observe the principle of "less is more."

Usage notes: Blush should be applied where your own cheek color naturally appears. Use a light touch: it's easier to add more if necessary than to remove excess. Cheek color that's barely enhanced should be your goal. Apply along bottom of cheekbone, beginning at an imaginary line running down from the center or the outside edge of your iris (difference will depend upon where your natural cheek color begins), blending upward just to the top edge of your cheekbone and outward toward hairline. Don't go closer than indicated toward your nose or farther up into the eye socket. If you go down too far or cover too large an area, your face will look heavy and drooping. Blend carefully so there are no definite edges to the color.

Eyes

There is a broad range of choice here in what you might use—from none to all. Note, please, that while every aspect of a Christian's makeup should be subtle, *the more enhancers you use the more subtle should be their application.* Otherwise, one + another + another = too much.

Eyes are the "windows of the soul." We who know Christ as Savior want always to let the spiritual beauty of a blood-cleansed heart shine through those windows. Since eyes are the most direct portals to and indicators of our personality, character, and soul, they should be the focal point of our faces. If you decide to give your eyes a bit of help cosmetically, any such aid should be so delicately applied that it never calls attention to itself but instead simply and subtly enhances. That immediately rules out the brazen, heavy-handed application seen in advertisements! Too, as you consider your eyes, do a bit of check-up: what state of soul do your eyes reveal? What spirit toward others looks out through them? If either of those is unlovely, external attempts to beautify your eyes are vain.

Eyes should be the central attraction in any human face because they're the main means of heart communication. Some eyes are naturally vivid and magnetic because of their shape and color. Many of us, though, have eyes that can stand a boost in interest.

Eyebrows. Brows create the frame for our eyes. Many eyebrows need a bit of shaping. That doesn't mean you change their distinctive shape; you define it by plucking extraneous hairs or darkening the brows. Always work for the most natural look in your eyebrows, both in color and shape.

There is a "formula" for rightly defining eyebrow shape. Hold a pencil or another straightedged object alongside your nose and running up to your brow line. Your eyebrows' inner ends should start there. If you have stray hairs growing farther toward the center, tweeze them: too-close brows create a perpetual frown. Brows too far apart, however, make you look startled. Next, holding the bottom of your straightedge against your nostril, pivot the top portion over the center of your eye as you look straight ahead into the mirror. Where it meets the brow should be the peak of your eyebrow's arch. If there are hairs on the under side of the brow making the arch indistinct, pluck them away. (Do not pluck brows from above.) Finally, still holding your measuring instrument against your nostril, pivot the top on to the outer corner of your eye: that's where the brow should end. If extra hairs march away toward cheek or hairline, tweeze them.

As for how much plucking to do in any of the areas mentioned, the answer is as little as possible—remove only "strays" that make the brow shape indistinct.

If your eyebrows are sparsely haired or pale in color, defining help comes in pencil or powder form. Stay close to your own color, or choose a neutral such as taupe. Pencil gives the less natural look, so if you prefer pencil, work very carefully with short strokes, then brush to blend. When applying powder color, fill in the brow with a small brush. When using either means of eyebrow color, aim for a natural look: brows are not a solid mass; they're a collection of fine, short individual hairs. That's the appearance you need to enhance or reproduce.

Eye shadow. Shadow works to accent and contour the eye area. When properly applied, shadow can make your eyes appear brighter. It gives dimension, shape, and depth to their appearance. Eye shadow comes in cream, stick, and pressed and dry powder form and in many colors. Sources recommend powder shadows as being easiest to use and most natural in appearance: that means neutral or earth tones—nothing bright or garish. It also means a light touch in application and very careful blending.

Don't use contour color that's the same as your eye color: complementary color enhances your own. Blue eyes are accented by peach, mauve, and neutrals (taupe or camel). Green eyes get a lift from rusts, coppers, and plums. Brown eyes sparkle when contoured with greens, grays, or blues. Here's how it's done:

Slightly lighter foundation on the eyelid and up to the brow "opens" the eyes area.

Contour color should simply accent natural shadow produced by the flesh that covers the orbital bone. Examine your eyes in the mirror; you'll see where the natural shadow falls.

If you have flesh that hangs down from the orbital bone onto your lid (and may even touch the lash line), don't try to use contouring.

Eye liner. Liner, too, comes in several forms: pencil, liquid, cake and felt-tip pens. Liner should be applied right at the lash line. It "opens" your eye making it look larger, and it also makes lashes appear to be thicker. Color that's closest to mascara color or a neutral works best for a blended look. Carefully consider your natural coloring; stay close to it in choosing eyeliner and mascara color. Black on a light blonde would be ill chosen. With eyeliner you can also define eye shape, and with careful use of liner you can equalize the size of eyes. Do not outline the entire eye—it gives the impression of a mask. Liner should begin at the iris and extend to the outer corner. Although it's called a "liner," don't let it be a line. An indistinct smudged accent is the goal.

Usage note: Don't use eyeliner on your eyes' inner rims (inside the lash line). Such placement poses the risk of infection.

Mascara. Some brunettes have eyelashes that are naturally dark enough to be seen along their entire length. Most of us, though, are not so agreeably endowed. Therefore, to remove lashes from the colorless and nondescript category, you may choose to use mascara. This product defines, darkens, thickens, and lengthens lashes. It may take the form of cake, liquid, or cream. The key word for its application is *sparingly.* Use a slow wiggling motion from eyelash base to tips. Concentrate color on the outer half of the eye for an open-eyed look.

Usage notes: If you curl your eyelashes, do so before applying mascara. Using a curler afterwards may break or pull out your lashes. When using the curler, clamp it on the lashes a couple of times rather than just once—first as close as possible to their base, then farther toward the ends. Single clamping can make lashes look bent instead of curled. (If you don't use mascara, curling alone can help give your eyes a brighter look, and Vaseline on your eyelashes will accent them.)

In using *any* mascara, avoid the "glop and top" method of application. Eyelashes are delicate individual *hairs,* and when they're defined by mascara, they should by all means still look like hairs—not like baling wires freshly dipped in creosote! Use an eyelash comb to separate lashes after applying mascara.

A parting note on eyelashes: be sure to remove every particle of mascara at the end of a day. Use a facial cleanser or a remover that's specially formulated for mascara. Leftover lash darkener is singularly unlovely, and it smudges on cheeks, pillows, and bath linens. Moreover, it serves as a poor base for tomorrow morning's fresh application.

General Eye Appearance

The characteristics that mark beautiful eyes are size, depth, spacing, and luminosity. In camouflaging less-than-pleasing eye characteristics, apply the principle of lighter for emphasizing and enlarging, darker for downplaying and reducing. Close-set eyes, for example, can be given an appearance plus by putting light base or concealer on the sides of the nose between your eyes.

Lips

Lip pencil. A pencil is a practical first step in applying lip color because it not only defines but also helps to keep lip color from "bleeding" into skin around the lips. (This becomes more important as you age and wrinkles increase and deepen.) Don't use a lip pencil that's greatly different from lipstick color. Experts suggest a matching color or one shade deeper. Outline your lips carefully with the pencil. It's in using lip pencil, too, that you can modify lip shape and size. If your lips are thin, apply line on outside edges. If you have lips that are large, line them just inside natural lip lines. For short lips that give the mouth a pinched look, extend the lip line outward past their ends. To disguise a very wide mouth, stop lip line short of its natural end point. For uneven lips use the reducing or enlarging techniques just mentioned as needed on the mismatched lip areas.

Lipstick. The principle for lipstick use is simple: brighter lips make a brighter face. "Brighten" does not mean "loud!" Lipstick comes in many types and textures. Transfer-resistant formulas are the longest lasting, but they can have a drying effect. Long-wearing on the label means it should last four to six hours; good ones contain moisturizers (aloe or vitamin E). Frosted lipsticks shimmer due to reflecting ingredients. Matte formulas deliver color that's opaque. Cream-formula lipsticks contain some light waxes. Moisturizing lipsticks are smooth and shiny. Sheer or satin indications on the label usually mean there's high oil content; in this type, the gloss will be stronger than the color.

After reading through various sources searching for indications of subtlety and naturalness that would befit Christian women, I concluded that in general creamy formulas in "gentle" colors are best. The effects of high-gloss or frosted lipsticks call attention to themselves, thus stealing focus from the "soul windows"—one's eyes.

General Makeup Usage

It can't be said too often or with too much emphasis: a woman who knows the Lord must always be subtle in her use of makeup. When choosing and using it, think of its desired appearance as a whisper—never letting it get loud, as in a shout. Your face and the godly character that lights it should be what others see and remember—not the makeup on its surface.

Surely you understand that cosmetics manufacturers are forever trying to drum up more sales—so they create changing fashion looks. As a general rule, *don't adopt them.* Why? Because (a) they're too distinctive—calling attention to themselves—and (b) it's a waste of time, money, and effort because they're sure to be short-lived. Instead, know your own face and its needs, opt for the most subtle means possible to enhance God's gift, and maintain a look that's not only appropriate to your unique personality but also *makes a positive contribution to your visible testimony.*

While working on this manuscript, I had the opportunity to see a wondrous transformation. A friend who has worked as a makeup consultant came to our house one day for a special project. One of my students had appealed to me for help with her appearance. I wish you could see her "before" and "after" snapshots. Applying the principles in this chapter, my friend changed a sickly looking, discouraged college student in a ponytail to a glowing, sparkling-eyed young woman whose lovely dark hair framed her face with soft, feminine lines. Did she look painted? Not at all. Her natural beauty had been *revealed* in all her facial features.

Corrective Makeup

Artists will tell you that symmetry is one aspect of beauty. Symmetry results from correct proportion and comparative sizes. Enhancing your individual facial beauty may entail some makeup techniques that offset a lack of symmetry. Lest you look in the mirror and immediately focus unhappily on some facial feature(s) that violates the symmetry principle, come back to realistic encouragement by considering what Sir Francis Bacon noted in his essay *Of Beauty*:

> That is the best part of beauty, which a picture cannot express.
> There is no excellent beauty that hath not some strangeness in the proportion.

So don't despise that individualizing feature that somehow or other doesn't follow the norm. Instead, recognize it as an evidence of your uniqueness, and set about to incorporate it into an overall picture of loveliness. There are some principles we can apply to move toward that goal.

Facial Shape

There is a shape in facial structure that's considered best from an artistic standpoint: the oval. Actually, however, our faces come in a variety of shapes.

Your face fits one of the shapes illustrated. To determine which one, pull back your hair and cover it with a towel to expose the outline of your face. Look squarely into the mirror. If necessary, use a piece of soap to draw the different shapes on your mirror, and move so that your face appears inside one after the other. It's important to know the natural shape of your face because your goal in makeup, hair styling, and perhaps even a bit in your wardrobe will be to give your face the appearance of being oval.

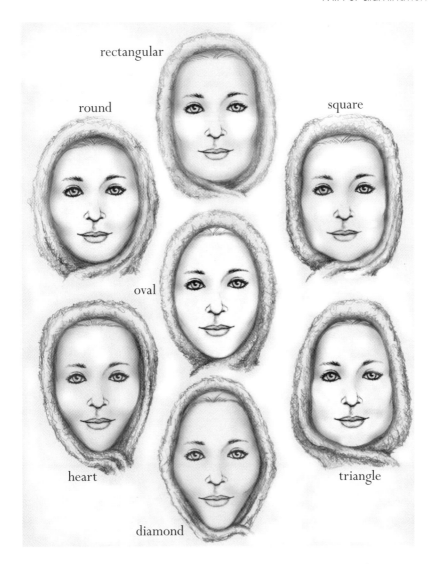

rectangular

round

square

oval

heart

triangle

diamond

Proportion

There is also an "ideal" arrangement of facial features. All of us have eyes, nose, and mouth in generally similar locations. But the face that is most pleasing to the eye has its individual features at certain relative distances from each other. It is from this proportional scaling that such terms as "long chin" or "high forehead" arise:

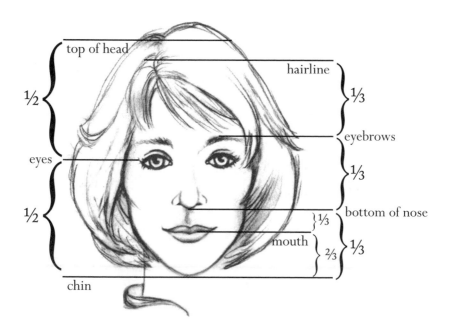

The basic tool for corrective cosmetics is make-up base in three tones: the one best matching your own complexion, a slightly lighter shade, and a slightly darker shade. With these three shades you can "model" the shape of your face.

The skin-matching foundation should be applied first over the entire face. Then begins any modeling that's needed. As has been mentioned earlier, dark recedes (or minimizes), while light advances (or emphasizes). Therefore, for an area of a face that is overly prominent or proportionately unpleasing, you would use the darker tone for correction. Conversely, if there is an area lacking desirable prominence, length, or width, you would apply the lighter.

To illustrate, here are some examples of corrective base application:

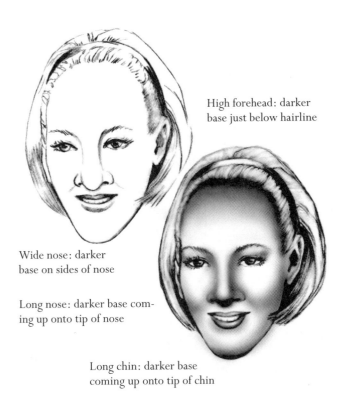

High forehead: darker
base just below hairline

Wide nose: darker
base on sides of nose

Long nose: darker base coming up onto tip of nose

Long chin: darker base
coming up onto tip of chin

*Any corrective use of cosmetics depends upon careful blending for its effective-
ness.* Lines of demarcation where one tone stops and another begins draw
attention and kill illusion. After your initial blending, check the effect in
natural light (daylight, preferably, but by all means something *other than*
fluorescent), particularly examining the side view, and blend again.

Eyeglasses

Need eyeglasses make your eyes unattractive? No! Some of the pret-
tiest eyes I've ever seen have smiled out from behind corrective lenses.
Moreover, designers and manufacturers of optical frames are doing great
things for making them flattering. Wisely chosen eyeglasses can add in-
triguing individuality to your appearance rather than detract from it.
Actually, a woman looks much better in well-chosen glasses than she does
in contact lenses if the contacts make her squint, blink, and frown.

Those of us whose vision needs a bit of help have plenty of company. The eyeglass industry reports that 60 to 70 percent of adults in America need corrective lenses. And for more than 80 percent of those, spectacles are required rather than contact lenses.

Opticians make and fit glasses. Some states allow them to dispense contact lenses. They cannot write prescriptions or diagnose and treat eye diseases. *Optometrists* hold postcollege degrees in optometry (OD). Though they don't perform surgery, they do eye examinations, diagnose diseases of the eye, and prescribe corrective lenses. Some states also let them prescribe drugs for eye diseases. *Ophthalmologists* are medical doctors in whose residency they've studied, diagnosed, and treated eye diseases. They can perform eye surgery.

Materials. Eyeglass lenses are available in glass or plastics and frames in metal or plastic. The various types of each have their own characteristics, advantages, and drawbacks. Lenses may be monovision, bifocal, trifocal, or progressive. There are also options for antireflection lenses, those with UV protection, and photochromic lenses that darken automatically in sunlight.

Designs. Design is the point at which confusion can set in. There are so many designs in eyeglass frames that the choice of a frame may seem daunting. There are, however, principles that can guide toward the best choice. They have to do with face shape, face size, and coloring of eyes, skin, and hair. Here's how they work.

Face Shape

In general, eyeglass frames should contrast with the shape of your face.

Oval. Many styles look good on this face. Frames should be as wide as or wider than the broadest part of the face. Try either rounded or geometric frames.

Round. Squared frames or angular, narrow frames help lengthen the face. Frames should be wider than they are deep. And a clear bridge will make the eye area seem wider.

Square. Narrow frame styles make the face look longer, and they soften the angles. Frames should also have more width than depth. Also try narrow ovals.

Rectangle. Frames need top-to-bottom depth. Decorative or contrasting temples add width. If your nose is long, look for glasses with a low bridge.

Diamond. Good frames for this face shape are those with detailed, distinctive brow lines. Rimless frames, oval, or cat-eye shapes can also work.

Triangle. Frames may have heavy color accents, decorative details on the top half of the frame, or cat-eye shapes.

Heart. Try frames that widen at the bottom. Light materials and colors and rimless styles are also good.

Face Size

Be very careful when considering proportion. Eyeglasses can overpower your face by being too large, and they seem lost if they're too small. Neither enhances your appearance, no matter how stylish they may be.

Coloring

Everyone looks best within her own sphere of colors. Warm coloring (yellow-based or peaches-and-cream) can wear frames of gold, khaki, camel, peach, orange, copper, coral, off-white, warm blue, or blond tortoise. Cool coloring (blue-based; olive is also included) would be wise to choose darker tortoise, jade, magenta, plum, blue gray, or black.

Whatever your face shape, face size, or coloring, you're wise to avoid the most "in" look when choosing eyeglasses. Instead, opt for classics. Otherwise, you'll soon have a dated appearance.

Further Details on Eyeglasses

Be sure your glasses fit properly. They shouldn't slide down your nose or move around with your changing facial expressions. Your eye should be centered in the frame. If the bridge of your nose "disappears" by nature, choose frames that have a bold bridge. The top of the frame should be just below your brow line.

Treat eyeglasses carefully—they're a considerable investment. Use both hands to put on and remove glasses. The one-handed technique can bend the temples and ruin the "sit" of the glasses. Never rest eyeglasses on their lenses. Instead, lay them down on the upper edge of the frame. Clean lenses carefully with a specially treated cloth, liquid lens cleaner, or mild soap and water.

Contact Lenses

If you're able to wear them, realize at the outset that contact lenses are going to cost more than eyeglasses. Too, you're also going to need a pair of glasses anyway as alternatives to use in case of problems with your contacts, to rest your eyes, or to find that contact that slips out of your hand.

Considerable improvements have been made to contact lenses. They're safer and more comfortable, and they offer better visual correction than earlier ones.

While most contact lenses are clear, colored ones are also available, though of course they're more expensive. If you choose color, go for the enhancement of your own eye color rather than one that greatly changes your color or has what I call a "neon" effect of unrealism.

- Only wear contacts that are fitted and prescribed by a licensed eye care professional.
- Don't buy contact lenses anywhere but from an authorized vendor. The FDA has issued a warning about the risk of permanent eye injury and blindness from lenses used without prescriptions and proper fitting. Such contacts may be sold through beauty salons, video and record stores, convenience stores, flea markets, and so forth.
- Always wash your hands before handling contacts.
- Don't swim while wearing contacts. The risk of infection is high.
- Carefully clean and store lenses according to your doctor's instructions.
- Never swap or share contacts with anyone.
- Don't sleep with contacts in your eyes unless they're extended-wear types designed for doing so.

Hair

A woman's "crowning glory" may also be her crowning grumble factor. One's hair can be a challenge not only in terms of its best health and care but also in terms of attractive styling. A woman's hair serves as a frame for her face; a poorly chosen frame can be one of the stealthiest, most successful thieves of her attractiveness.

We don't know what Eve did with her hair. Doubtless it was luxuriantly healthy and ideal in its framing of her face; those would be perfect characteristics in keeping with the garden's perfection. Woman's fuss with hair probably started as soon as Eden's gate swung shut.

The modern preoccupation with hair care, color, and styling really isn't modern at all, and hair care attention hasn't just been for women; men have been active therein, as well. Imagination has been heartily applied by both genders.

Egyptian combs made from dried fish bones date back to the fifth century B.C. The people of the Nile also made shampoo and conditioner. In the second century B.C., Babylonian men of high rank used gold dust to powder their hair. Assyrian kings and noblemen had their hair curled with heated iron bars. Cleopatra is credited with introducing hair ornaments in 35 B.C., when she wore bejeweled ivory pins in her hair. Both bleaching and darkening of hair were practiced in Roman times. Even warfare sometimes involved hair: Saxons would appear on the battlefield sporting bright green, orange, and blue hair—apparently to frighten the enemy. In the Middle Ages women in Europe used lizards boiled in olive oil for conditioning their hair. They also created high foreheads by shaving their hairlines in front. And of course the towering, fantastic hairstyles of seventeenth- and eighteenth-century France are legendary for the extremes that caused their wearers all sorts of difficulties and discomforts.

And so hairstyling efforts and effects have gone on through the years. The first public hair salon for ladies opened in Paris in 1635. And two hundred years later beauty parlors opened in the United States. In 1905 Charles Nestle invented the first permanent wave machine. The first chemical hair color formula came into being in 1907; it ultimately became L'Oreal. The first hair dryer was invented in 1920.

The ever-changing styles of women's hair aren't just the result of individual fancy; there is also a fascinating connection with and reflection of changing social atmospheres within historical periods.

So much for a peek into hair history; now to present and personal hair considerations. What about following current fashion trends in hair? One season curly is "in"; the next it's nothing but ruler-straight locks wherever you look; then it's short or long, pouffy or flat. Applying the principle of balance which is so important in the Christian life, stick to a general outline that is best for your face, body proportions, and features. Within that outline, have the imaginative flexibility to adapt your hairstyle so that it has just a hint of what's current. A case in point has been the hold-on-to-the-death attitude of some Christian women with bouffant hairstyles. All that back-combing and high-piling were so hopelessly outmoded by the blow-dry and curling-iron era that those who clung to them made spectacles of themselves. It is not wise to gallop along trying to keep up with every little spurt of fashion—but neither is it wise to be so far behind with a years-gone-by hairdo that those seeing you react with "Ohhh, brother!" or "Yuck!" A woman should wear that which fits her lifestyle, expresses her personality, and is compatible with her hair type. Teens, it's not wise to adopt a style worn by a model, entertainment figure, or friend. Why be a poor copy rather than a fine original? You need to wear your hair in such a way that it is a *plus* for your appearance, not a *minus*.

First of all, consider what type of frame your face needs. Correct hair styling can do a great deal to make your face appear more oval and give the illusion of ideal proportions. Following is a gleaning of hairstyle options. In each case you should also consider your personality, adapting the basic features of proportion to it.

Oval

- Most styles will work on this shape

Round

- Volume on top, less on sides

- Short, fringy cut brushed forward toward face
- Side part running in a diagonal to crown
- Wispy bangs or none
- No center part

Square
- No blunt, jaw-length cuts
- No straight bangs; but tapered
- Overall softness, some height at crown
- Volume away from sides
- Asymmetrical styles are good

Rectangle
- Short or chin-length cuts
- Fullness at sides
- Bangs
- No center part
- No unnecessary height

Triangle
- Fullness at top
- Full at upper sides
- Soft bangs
- Asymmetrical bangs
- Soft waves and curls that direct attention above eye line

Heart
- Add width at jaw line
- Softness covering ears
- Fullness at nape of neck
- No center part
- Flippy ends work well
- Blunt cuts work well
- Avoid either too-flat or too-high styling

Diamond
- No fullness at eye line

- Fullness high and low
- Softness in styling is best

You should also consider your height, weight, and body type so that your hairstyle is in keeping with your overall appearance proportionately.

Tall

- No too-short cuts
- Avoid long, straight, droopy styles
- Medium length allowing for soft fullness is good

Athletic

- Neat
- Softly waved rather than fluffy or curly
- Not too tight to head

Petite

- No "big hair" look; it overpowers

There is one aspect of hair that is uniquely a concern of Christian women: its *length*. Some believers feel very strongly that hair should be long. Indeed, the Bible speaks of a woman's hair as her "crown," her "covering." Ah, but then comes the question "What is long?" We can't simply say "longer than a man's," because there are some time-warp sixties men who wear their hair so long it would be a tremendous feat to out-grow them.

In today's society, hair is classified as long if it passes the midpoint of the neck. Some Christians feel that only waist- or hip-length hair can suffice as "long." A genuine conviction in this matter is certainly to be honored. At the same time, however, we need to be sure that "conviction" is not a convenient cover term for legalism, self-righteousness, or pride. I have known many girls and women whose flowing tresses in no way offset their frozen charity.

Length of hair is really not the only consideration of how a Christian should choose a style. There's also the visual impression: for example, a short hairstyle can either be feminine or mannish in its appearance.

There is another consideration for correctly choosing a hairstyle: age. Long, loose-flowing hair (if it's clean, shining, and healthy) can be beautiful in itself and flattering throughout girlhood and perhaps into one's early twenties. After that, however, the visual effects move into the negative zone. Why? Because long hanging hair is a *down* line—and that's the worst possible addition to the down-pull of aging. If you keep wearing your hair long as a youth wannabe, because your husband likes it, or you feel there is something spiritual about it, counteract the down lines; adopt a style (at least for appearance in public) that gives an upward line, a visual lift to your face.

Likewise, the little-girl look of hair bows and so forth needs to be left behind. Not long ago my husband and I were in a church congregation when a middle-aged woman entered and sat several rows ahead of us. Her hair was entirely gray; it not only hung loose down past her shoulders but it also sported a cutesy bow on one side. My husband leaned over and said, "That poor lady! Why doesn't someone help her with her appearance?"

No on can retain or recapture her youth; trying to do so in one's appearance just creates a tragi-comic effect.

Whatever style you adopt because of its maximum flattery, do start with a good cut. Poorly cut hair doesn't cooperate with your needs and wants. When you look for a good cosmetologist, it's wiser to ask for one who *handles your type of hair well* rather than simply asking for a talented stylist. A good haircut doesn't come from chopping and lopping; it has to do with shaping—and that in turn depends much upon hair textures and curl characteristics. Before you let the operator put scissors or razor to your hair, tell her exactly what result you want (don't be loathe to show her a picture); explain the difficulties you may have encountered in styling your hair; get her advice—as to the practicality of the style for your hair and on how best to prepare your hair for styling after its basic cut.

In order to maintain your well-cut hair at its shining, attractive best, you might need to have quite a collection of hair products that are formulated for your hair type, such as creme rinse, conditioner, volumizer, setting lotions, and so forth. But they will be well paid for in the increased ease and effectiveness in hair handling. The compliments you may get will be nice; but the greatest benefit will come as people see that being a Christian does *not* mean having limp, stringy hair and a bedraggled look.

Another aspect due our consideration regarding hair is its color. Young hair is lovely in all of its natural hues. But hair, like all our other physical parts, changes with age: it drabs, it darkens, or it grays. Some women darken or gray beautifully; the change actually enhances their skin and their eyes. But for others, the change moves us toward "blah." When that happens, you may opt for color treatment.

There are different types of hair color products: temporary rinses, semipermanent tints, dyes for darkening, bleach or color treatments for lightening, and highlighting. If you decide to go for permanent hair coloring, I'd strongly advise you to turn the project over to a qualified operator. There are just too many pitfalls threatening the do-it-yourselfer. Among them are too-dark, too-light, uneven color, color variations from application to application, damaged hair, missed spots . . . As in the other areas we've considered, hair color for a Christian woman should not only add to her appearance; it should also be subtle and natural looking. Minute differences in color can make major differences in your appearance—good or bad.

There is one final factor to consider in connection with hairstyles; appropriateness. Interestingly, secular texts emphasize this point.

The way you choose to wear your hair at a particular time should take into consideration the nature of your activity at that time. While working in a professional setting, for example, your hair should have a smooth, neat, unfussy appearance. That look correctly says "business." Evening social occasions, on the other hand, provide an opportunity for the more fancy hairstyles we enjoy now and then. That look says "dress up."

By the time you reach this point in the chapter, some of you may be thinking, "I'm a housewife with three kids and a hectic schedule! There's no time for all this!" The overwhelming majority of us can raise similar protests. But how does either the domestic or professional status rule out paying attention to the overall picture we present each day to those around us?

It needn't take you *long* to make yourself look presentable first thing in the morning. As stewards of the Lord's time and carriers of numerous and extensive responsibilities, our make-up and hair routine should occupy only a ten-to-twenty-minute time slot from start to finish. But those minutes are important! They're important first of all to the eyes of our family members because of the message they convey: we care (or don't care) enough about those we love to look good for them. Second, they're important to our visible testimony in the world at large. And finally, they are important to our own eyes: seeing a pale, droopy self in the mirror lowers our spirits, discourages us mentally, and sucks joyfulness out of our daily living.

I want to add an extra note for you who are married. Was the fine print on your marriage certificate a license to disintegrate in your appearance? Did your husband leave his eyes at the altar? Does he live now in a cave where there are no well-groomed, lovely women around him each day? Rather than letting marriage (whether three months or fifty-three years long) be an excuse against maintaining a good appearance, it should be a strong motivation for it! The greatest compliment a woman can pay her husband is to keep herself attractive for him.

Spiritual X-Rays

Take heed to yourselves, that your heart be not deceived, and ye turn aside, and serve other gods, and worship them.

As you read this chapter, did you congratulate yourself for doing things correctly in using makeup and choosing a hairstyle? If your self-evaluation is accurate, that's okay. But—did your mind go to someone else with a scornful or condemning air toward her? If so, you just turned ugly! Back up and rethink. She doesn't need to do or not do as you've chosen. You are supposed to love her as she is, for who she is.

The preceding pages have necessarily dealt with facial surfaces and their frame and techniques for enhancing them. Wouldn't it be wonderful, though, if each Christian woman or girl had a face like that of Moses when he came down from Mount Sinai?

And it came to pass, when Moses came down from mount Sinai with the two tables of testimony in Moses' hand, when he came down from the mount, that Moses wist not that the skin of his face shone. **Exod. 34:29**

Moses had spent forty days and forty nights in the presence of Jehovah. That, surely, was the ultimate beautification for any mortal! While of course we could never expect to duplicate Moses' experience, we can desire its spiritual parallel. Our time spent in personal communication with God through Bible study and prayer should so warm our soul that our face radiates the joyful privilege of that meeting. In such reality, Christian lady, is the truest, most exalted beauty any one of us can have.

So, now that we have examined our faces and hairstyles, we need to do an even more careful study of something else: our carpet. Carpet? Right. The desire of the Christian woman should be *total loveliness*. Powder and paint cannot long hide a shallow brain or a sickly soul. So examine your carpet. Where does it show greater wear: where you pray, or where you preen? Rightly, of course, it should be the former. If not, that's where the most earnest corrective measures need to be taken! If your spiritual life is pale and unlovely, the mirror you need to use more is that of God's Word. "Beauty is only skin deep" should never be truthfully applied to a born-again Christian woman. Not a single day should pass when we don't spend time beautifying our souls.

Generation Considerations

Teens

Let no man despise thy youth; but be thou an example of the believers, in word, in conversation, in charity, in spirit, in faith, in purity.

I repeat what was said early in this chapter: don't wear any makeup unless or until you have to—and when that time comes, wear as little as possible. In hair, too, keep to simplicity: this is the one time in your life it will work splendidly for you. Too much makeup and color-treated or overdone styling of hair makes you look hardened.

Mothers

That our daughters may be as corner stones, polished after the similitude of a palace.

Preparation for the right kind of makeup usage needs to start long before teenage years arrive. Even as your little girl plays with dolls, direct her toward appreciation of and liking for the right "look." Specifically, for example, I think of the contrast between Barbie dolls and American Girl dolls. You might point out the stiff, painted look of a Barbie and extol the lovely naturalness of the American Girl characters. Both, of course, have painted faces—but the difference is evident!

Mentors

Shewing to the generation to come the praises of the Lord, and his strength, and his wonderful works that he hath done.

Your positive input can weigh heavily in this matter. Encourage mothers when you see them rightly guarding and guiding their daughters. Encourage girls about their sweet looks in their natural state. They may be getting pulled and pushed into a too-early, false "maturity" from other sources. Your warm, genuine admiration can be an anchor against the contrary forces.

Caution Lights

Take heed therefore that the light which is in thee be not darkness.

The care and dressing of a woman's face is an area in which Christians can become extremely judgmental, even getting into the use of unkind labels and name calling. Emphasis throughout the chapter has been on the testimony value of appearance. Exactly how that transfers into personal preference will vary greatly among individuals—and that's as it should be. God doesn't make us walk single file in our minor life choices. He instead always sees and focuses on the internals. We should do the same. We're to *love* our neighbor, not shun, dislike, or condemn her because her appearance differs from ours.

CHAPTER SEVEN

Spotlighting Gracefulness

CHAPTER SEVEN

Spotlighting Gracefulness

Blessed is the people that know the joyful sound: they shall walk, O Lord, in the light of thy countenance. **Ps. 89:15**

are you finished enhancing your loveliness for the Lord's sake when you've carefully attended to face and hair? Not by a long shot, though you might judge otherwise by the careless physical bearing of many women. Posture and carriage deposit to or withdraw from our personal appearance accounts.

Excluding professionally oriented training classes and special "finishing" schools, emphasis upon graceful carriage is almost nonexistent in our day. This lack is sadly evident all the time and in every place across the nation; its results, though, are especially regrettable in Christian women. Of all women, we who know Christ as Savior should be exemplary in our physical bearing as a means of reflecting the Creator's original design. His plan was that we should be upright in posture and carriage. But just as humanity has departed spiritually from His intention, so too have we individuals departed physically.

There are several reasons for a born-again girl or woman to excel in posture and carriage.

We are daughters of the King of glory. That wonderful truth surely draws your heart upward with gratitude, doesn't it? Erect physical bearing much better reflects internal uprightness than does slouching carriage.

We are to serve as magnets for and mirrors of our Lord. Imagining an unbelieving woman's absence of hope and joy in our dark world, it's not difficult to understand why she would slump or slink. The *difference* of our erect, gracefully feminine carriage can draw her to ask us the reason for that difference.

We should seek to fulfill the Lord's intention for femininity: the beauty of holiness. The more the world screams "Unisex!" by dress, carriage, and actions, and the more its inhabitants evidence the downward pull of their spiritual darkness, the more clearly does each of us need a graceful, womanly posture and carriage that makes a silent statement against the dark spirit of the age.

Each of us has the responsibility, as God's child, to obey His command for modesty. Knowledge of and practice in proper carriage helps immeasurably in maintaining modesty.

The Holy Spirit's indwelling of our body as His temple makes it imperative that we take the best possible care of it. Good posture is a positive factor in good health. Good physical carriage affords the right framework for healthy heart and lungs, thus contributing to energy and stamina. Poor posture can worsen menstrual cramps, create backache, and cause headaches.

With that spiritual foundation laid for our discussion, we're ready to move on to examine physical grace in its various components.

Standing

Good posture is basically *upright stance.* Look at a toddler's posture. It's beautiful! The little back is straight, the chest high, the head erect. But as the child grows, she learns by example to "crumple" in her posture. The main crumple time often strikes in the junior high school years, for several reasons:

- rapid physical growth and the accompanying feeling of awkwardness

- a developing bosom to hide
- an undeveloped bosom to hide

Very soon, poor posture becomes habitual. And therein lies the problem: our grown-up carriage (usually poor) is a habit. It's a bad habit that should be replaced.

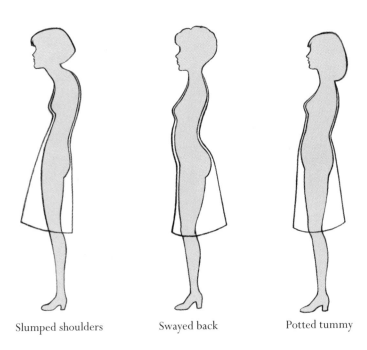

Slumped shoulders   Swayed back   Potted tummy

Sketches are one thing, but reality is infinitely better (or worse). And it's most effective if you make the illustration personal. Stand so that you can see your side view in a full-length mirror. Which one of the sketched poor postures does your *habitual* stance most closely resemble? (Don't cheat and "pull up" for this analytical look!) Awful? Well, then, grit your teeth, ask for the Lord's help, and set out to replace bad habits with good ones.

The key to good posture is proper body alignment. When standing correctly, a body's side view can have an imaginary straight line drawn down its length from head to feet. Study the alignment diagram below and correct your posture accordingly. Note, too, that the position of your feet is important. A wide-track stance lacks grace.

Head—chin parallel to the floor (neither raised, "snooty," nor lowered, "defeated"); ears riding directly over shoulders

Shoulders—back and down, relaxed rather than stiff; not "military" (to find proper position: with rib cage high, raise shoulders as far toward the ears as possible, then let them relax into a down-and-back position)

Neck—upright, a straight column rising from the shoulders; neither thrust forward nor craned backward

Chest—lifted out of belt line (imagine a string attached to your breastbone, pulling your rib cage toward the ceiling)

Back—straight and tall, having only a very slight natural curve at waist

Tummy—pulled in absolutely flat. Here, you really may have let your muscles "go to pot"! Don't let them stay there. Retrain and keep them in tone. A pulled-in tummy instantly takes pounds off your appearance. It also contributes to a healthy lower back.

Derriere—the pelvis (bony girdle onto which your legs are hinged) should be tipped so the buttocks are tucked somewhat under. This does away with the "big back porch" look.

Knees—slightly flexed; not locked and stiff

Feet—weight evenly distributed between balls and heels. Feet should be parallel to each other with toes pointed neither out nor in.

You may feel uncomfortable when your body is properly aligned. Don't be discouraged, and certainly don't give up and revert to slovenly carriage. The longer you've practiced poor posture, the harder it will be to break your bad habits. But the improvement, not only in the way you look but also in the way you feel, will make your efforts happily worthwhile.

By *posture alone* a woman can make a $200 dress look like a grab-bag reject. Conversely, erect carriage can make a $2 bargain look expensive. To convince yourself of this fact, put any one of your outfits on a dress form adjusted to your measurements. Notice how attractively the dress fits and hangs. Now put it on your *own* form, and assume your habitual posture.

See how you alter the whole visual effect? Makes you wonder which one is the dummy, doesn't it?

Correcting poor posture habits may take long, hard work; at first it will mean checking up on your body alignment every little while all through the day every day: when any one section or the whole regresses into unlovely old ways, pull everything back into proper alignment.

Here's a special reminder for pregnant women. Don't sacrifice the tonicity of your stomach muscles by just letting them go limp during those nine months. Keep your tummy muscles working at the support project. It will not only help to offset backache while you're pregnant; it will also put you a good step ahead in recovering your prepregnancy figure.

Work for *consistently* good posture—not just a "know-how-to-but-only-use-on-special-occasions" type. The harder, more faithfully you strive to overcome poor habits, the sooner they'll be replaced by good ones. Oh—and don't let tiredness be an excuse. In fact, the more tired you are, the more important good posture is! Case in point: pick a time you feel you've expended every ounce of energy; now pull up into your tallest, straightest posture, take the time to draw several long, full breaths into your newly uncramped lungs, and feel how some of the exhaustion lifts. Multiply that effect by consistent proper bearing throughout the day, and you've provided for yourself a generous boost toward increased physical energy and efficiency.

Walking

Actually, walking is not a separate consideration, for proper carriage is simply good posture *put into action*. There are five things to think about as you analyze and improve your walk.

First, the body should appear unified in its walking: smooth, coordinated, and graceful. Your best private teacher for this aspect of your training would be a candid video of your habitual walk. Watch the recorded action carefully: is there jerkiness, turkey-head movement, or other characteristics of poor carriage? If that kind of off-guard self observation isn't available, watch your walk in a few plate glass store windows.

The only parts of your body that should show any appreciable move-ment in walking are your legs and arms. Head and shoulders should be motionless. Arms are to swing naturally at the sides—slightly curved and relaxed, not stiff and militaristic. They move in opposition to the legs: when the right leg is forward, the left arm is forward and vice versa.

As for the legs themselves, the walking movement ideally comes from the thighs down. Legs should swing *from* the hips—without the hips themselves swaying. A woman naturally has a bit more movement in the hip area than does a man, due to physical structure (thigh bone/pelvis attachment is different); a born-again woman, however, must not have a pronounced "movie star" swish of the hips! Such a walk is inextricably connected to the "Come on, boys," freewheeling sexual attitude of the world. If there is too much hip movement in your walk, you're probably either walking with too little bending of your knees or with too long a stride. Either creates extra hip swing. But either can be corrected and thus eliminate the swivel-hips negative.

Second, the feet should fall in such a way that they skim either side of an imaginary line. If you try to walk with steps following each other directly *on* that line, you will look teetery. But keeping the inner side of each foot moving along beside the line makes your progress graceful rather than wide-track and ungainly.

Third, toes must remain parallel to each other throughout the walk. Toes pointing either out or in create an awkward appearance.

Fourth, your stride should be about the length of your shoe: that will prevent the too-long stride of a furrow-crossing field hand or too-short mincing steps.

Fifth, weight is constantly, smoothly shifted during walking. As you step forward, weight moves first onto the heel of the forward foot (but don't wham your weight down), moves smoothly onto the middle and ball of the foot, then springs forward off the toes as the other leg comes for-ward.

Pivoting

The pivot may be an item of graceful movement you've not considered, but adding it to your store of "moving knowledge" will contribute positively to your carriage.

A pivot is simply a turn: the most efficient and graceful method of turning. Practice the following description and diagram (this is a pivot to the right) until the pivot becomes second nature to you:

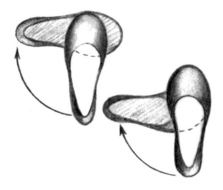

1. At the end of a line of walking, "close" with the rear (right, in this instance) foot—that is, bring the right toe forward until it is approximately on a plane with the left instep.
2. Shift weight onto the balls of the feet.
3. Lifting the heels of both feet slightly off the floor, turn to the right without lifting balls of feet from floor at all. Return heels to floor, and you're ready to move off at a right angle from your original line of walking.
4. In pivoting all the way around to go back in the direction from which you came, there will have to be an imperceptible lifting/sliding of the right foot as you pivot. Although it may seem complicated in print, the pivot technique is not really difficult. But if, after a fair number of attempts, you find that it feels stilted to you, by all means forget it! None of us should have a self-conscious, clothing-model appearance. The ideal is to practice the pivot *until it becomes the natural way for you to turn.*

Sitting

A simple chair can be an enemy to gracefulness. The challenge, however, is conquerable.

Many women instinctively recognize the enmity of chairs but capitulate and crumple into the sitting position in hopes that speed will camouflage awkwardness. Empty hopes! *Graceful control* is the key to proper sitting. *Avoid the ungainly practices of*

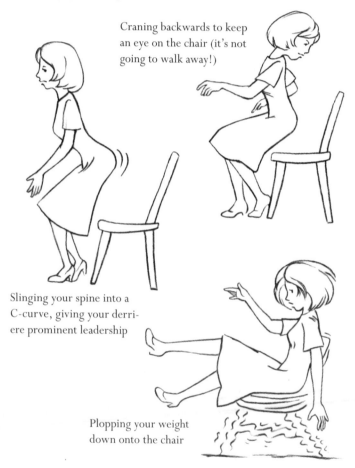

Craning backwards to keep an eye on the chair (it's not going to walk away!)

Slinging your spine into a C-curve, giving your derriere prominent leadership

Plopping your weight down onto the chair

The following steps for graceful sitting should be practiced until the entire movement is easy, natural, and habitual for you.

- Look at the chair as you approach it, checking its position and height.

- Stop looking at the chair; pivot gracefully in front of it.

- With your back to the chair, position one leg so that your calf touches the seat front. This provides a physical recheck of position and height.

- Keeping your *back straight* and your *head erect,* lower yourself *in one smooth movement* into the chair. Your thigh muscles should do almost all of the work; don't let them go off duty until you are satisfactorily seated. (If you discover that your thigh muscles have grown weak, incorporate daily parallel lunging exercises to whip them back into shape.)

- Allow your arms to hang at your sides as you sit; your hands can be unobtrusively straightening your skirt on your way down. (Don't grab the chair arms and heave yourself into position.)

- Once seated, as nearly as possible keep your body in a slight S-curve. Don't yank at your skirt, wriggle, twist, or otherwise make a production of finding a comfortable position.

- Hands are best placed when resting in your lap. Putting them on the chair arms makes you appear wide.

- Keep your back and head erect; sit on the bottom end of your spine—not slumped onto the middle or top of it.

- Cross your legs at the *ankles* rather than at the knees. Legs crossed at the knees can make a skirt or culottes grossly immodest; anyone sitting or standing to the front of you gets an unobstructed view. This is a frequent complaint made by Christian men—and rightly so. Even worse than the usual knee-crossing used by women is the unthinkable but increasingly common practice of crossing legs the way men do: with the ankle of one leg resting on the knee of the other leg.

- Finally, and this is a ***cardinal rule*** for the seated position: *keep knees and ankles together*! This point demands some extra concentration of thought, because violation of this causes extreme immodesty.

I would beg Christian women and girls to pay particular attention to those last two items involved in sitting correctly. There are uncounted times even in places intended to be the most spiritual—mission stations, church services, Sunday school sessions, Christian school classrooms—when women sitting carelessly are being crassly immodest. That ought never to be.

Special Challenges to Grace

Have you ever noticed how a simple accessory can undo graceful appearance? A case in point: a purse. So how do we carry a purse gracefully? The type with a moderate-sized handle or strap is best carried with your arm coming *from the outside in* through the strap(s). A small-handled bag, a clutch, or an envelope-type purse may be carried in your hand in the extended, normal standing or walking position or under your arm just above the elbow. A shoulder bag, of course, should live up to its design when you carry it—without making you walk with the weight-bearing shoulder high.

There are several actions that can make us feel and look particularly awkward: donning or discarding a coat, entering or exiting a car, getting seated at a picnic table, and picking up something from the floor or ground.

Putting on or removing a coat. Here's how to smooth the process when someone is helping you with the coat:

- Avoid backing and flapping like a retreating hen.
- Approach the coat face forward as it's held by your escort, visually checking its height.
- Put one arm into a sleeve.
- Pivot toward that arm.
- Bring other arm around behind you to the height of the leading arm, find armhole, and slip arm into it.
- Allow escort to lift coat onto your shoulders.
- Remove by reversing above actions.

And for those times when it's just you and the coat:

- Place one arm in coat; raise coat partially onto that arm and shoulder.
- Reach around back with the other arm and place it in the second coat sleeve.
- Pull coat up onto shoulders by both hands drawing lapels upward.
- Remove by dropping coat off one shoulder, allowing it to slide off that arm. Bring free arm around in front, grasp shoulder seam near collar as it slides off second arm. Place shoulder seams together, and hang the coat, folded, across one arm if you're not planning to put it on a hanger.

Although any description is necessarily disjointed, the actions can actually be molded into one smooth, fluid movement.

Entering and exiting a car.

- Sit first (two exceptions: the car is *very* little and low or you're entering the back seat of a two-door).
- Swing both legs up and into the car, in one smooth movement, *keeping knees and ankles together.*
- Exit by reversing the described movement.

The "exception" situations mentioned above can best be tackled by a step-forward-while-crouching technique. Understandably, such a maneuver won't win any awards for gracefulness—but it will get you into the car.

Sitting on table-attached picnic benches

- Set your food-laden plate down on the table.
- Step over the bench, one leg at a time, in the standing position (being careful to supervise your skirt).

Or

- Sit on bench with back toward the table; if wearing a skirt or culottes, gather the fabric closely around knees; swing both legs over simultaneously, *keeping knees and ankles together.*

Picking up an object from the floor or ground

- Do *not* bend from waist and hips, making yourself look like a stinkbug.

- *Do* keep your back straight. Bend at the knees, going into a deep knee bend with your thigh muscles powering the movement.

In the preceding few pages we have covered the basic principles for good posture and carriage. If the principles merely remain black squiggles on white sheets of paper, they won't do you an iota of good. But if you will transfer them to your mind and translate them into habitual body control, you will demonstrate the kind of feminine grace that states your delight in the Lord's crowning human creation—womanhood.

Spiritual X-Rays

Take heed to yourselves, that your heart be not deceived, and ye turn aside, and serve other gods, and worship them.

While considering your physical posture and carriage, realize that of far greater import is the uprightness of your inner woman. Do your ethics stand tall? Do you stoop to petty gossip? Do you slump into small deceits? Do you have a swaybacked character that "adjusts" to please whatever crowd you're with at a given moment? And what of your spiritual movement—is it *forward* for and toward the Lord? Do your soul's feet walk upon the distinctly drawn line of His holy Word? If the inner woman is not characterized by God's grace, physical grace is wasted.

Generation Considerations

Teens

Let no man despise thy youth; but be thou an example of the believers, in word, in conversation, in charity, in spirit, in faith, in purity.

Just as young skin and its color are blessings to be enjoyed, so too is a young, energetic, and limber body. Establishing proper habits of posture and carriage is much easier in your youth than later—when trying to undo habits is difficult because of lessened flexibility. The same is true of your mind and heart: how much better it is to make spiritual uprightness a habit now than to retrain a slouchy soul later.

Mothers

That our daughters may be as corner stones, polished after the similitude of a palace.

An important part of a girl's polishing is that of physical grace. For a few it comes naturally. For a greater number, however, it must be learned. And you, mother, are the most obvious choice to be the teacher. Begin while your daughter is very young—especially instructing her how to sit modestly. Then as she moves into puberty, go on to encourage her toward tall carriage and a smooth walk.

The spirit with which you carry out the instruction can make or break her learning: keep it positive and as lighthearted as possible. Nagging won't work; it will just make your daughter self-conscious and miserable. By the way, a junior high girl who knows the principles of good carriage has an advantage as she goes through those difficult years of transition.

Mentors

Shewing to the generation to come the praises of the Lord, and his strength, and his wonderful works that he hath done.

While working on this manuscript I lost a friend who had, unknowingly, mentored me for years in posture. Joyce was coming into her mid-seventies when she died—but her upright, energetic carriage unfailingly communicated youthfulness and a positive spirit. Just being around her made me want to stand up straight! The lovely tall carriage that marked her physically also reflected the inner woman: a godly, dedicated lifelong single whose lips and life brought honor to her Savior.

Whether single or married, you too can model gracefulness.

Caution Lights

Take heed therefore, that the light which is in thee be not darkness.

It's possible, of course, to make one's posture and carriage a fetish. The repeated urgings in preceding pages to make proper posture and carriage habitual have been written with a purpose beyond correctness and ease. Only grace of bearing and movement that are so much a habit that they seem ingrained can lack self-consciousness. That's an important point, be-cause self-awareness ruins the whole picture: it says "Look at me—I know how to do things!" That prideful attitude signals severe curvature of the spine spiritually.

CHAPTER EIGHT

Light and Sound

CHAPTER EIGHT

Light and Sound

To the law and to the testimony: if they speak not according to this word, it is because there is no light in them. **Isa. 8:20**

Oops, what's this subject—speaking—doing in here?" you may ask. The answer is that your speech is an integral part of the "picture" you present to the world. I've known more than a few women whose really lovely exteriors were nullified when they opened their mouths. The mouth provides clues to a woman's real self and influences others' reactions.

How about you? Does your voice, like fingernails scraping a chalkboard, cause people to shiver? Or do you frequently hear, "Pardon me, what was that you said?" Do your children comment that you always sound angry? If those or other negative reactions meet you in the everyday round of life, this chapter can prove especially beneficial to you. But all of us need to take time to think about our speech—its sound and its contents.

Sound

Most of us take our voices for granted. But our entire speech mechanism is a marvelous part of God's human creation. Human language and communication are gifts too easily devalued and misused.

Voices have several distinct characteristics; in order to make them really meaningful to you, you need to hear your own voice from the outside, as others do. Ask someone to make a recording of your speech when you're not aware of it. Then *really listen* to yourself. Also enlist the aid of two or three friends who love you enough and care sufficiently about the impression you make on other people to tell you the truth.

Now, keeping your voice recording handy, consider the quality of the sound you produce, its overall "feel." An unlovely quality grates on ears and nerves alike. Desirable characteristics are richness and *pleasantness*. William Shakespeare well described a lovely feminine voice in King Lear's line "Her voice was ever soft, gentle, and low—an excellent thing in woman." More importantly, remember that Scripture directs Christian women to have a "meek and quiet spirit"; harsh vocal quality belies such a spirit. Most of us need to strive to incorporate gentleness into our voices. But in trying to overcome vocal unpleasantness, don't change to a breathy, little-girl quality. Breathiness comes across as being phony or slightly unbright, neither of which serves as an attractive advertisement for Christianity!

Second, consider *projection*. How loudly or softly do you habitually speak? A loud-mouthed woman is a walking abomination. No matter how good her heart, she deafens and disgusts her poor hearers by her megaphone tones. Read through Proverbs and see how often loudness partly describes the wrong kind of woman. Loudness translates as brazenness— a far cry from the gentleness a born-again woman should convey! If you habitually speak too loudly, by all means relearn your vocal habits. Give the ears of your loved ones and acquaintances a well-deserved break. On the other hand, your projection shouldn't be so anemic that you sound sick and your "hearers" can't hear you.

Pitch is a third consideration. It has to do with the basic placement of your voice on a musical scale. There are, of course, great variations in habitual pitches from person to person. The extremes for a woman to avoid are the super-low voice whose huskiness comes across as a "whiskey" or "smoker's" voice, or the super-high voice that sounds like a mouse with its tail stepped on. Don't try to alter your basic pitch drastically, forcing yourself into an unnatural and uncomfortable register. But if you have an unpleasant pitch, a slight adjustment in habitual level can enhance your "listenability."

Pace is the fourth area in which we can work to improve our audible image. We should neither rattle at machine-gun rate nor drag so slowly through our sentences that listeners snore between words and phrases. The racing rate makes us sound brainless; the dragging rate communicates our being too lazy to live. Either end of the pace spectrum will cause listeners to turn us off—it's just not worth the effort!

Enunciation, or word formation, is the fifth and final aspect of vocal characteristics that need a check-up. We produce a wide range of speech sounds by minute adjustments in the jaw, lips, tongue, soft palate, and teeth. Most of us know how to form our sounds correctly; but we grow lazy and careless. For example, we often reduce -ing endings on words to -n'—as in runnin', comin', and so forth. Or we produce our consonants so carelessly that people find it hard to understand our words: e.g., "stan'art" for "standard." Perhaps, though, rather than laziness or carelessness, your particular problem is a regional dialect so thick it makes your speech unintelligible to hearers who speak General American. Whatever our shortcomings in enunciation, we need to spend some time and effort polishing them into acceptable, understandable form.

You can improve your vocal characteristics. Take the matter to the Lord, ask family and friends to remind you when your particular vocal fault creeps in, and practice, practice, practice the *best* voice you can produce. Use your travel time or housework hours; talk to the vacuum while you clean or to the bathtub while you scour. To multiply the effectiveness of your practice, use Scripture verses as your practice material; not only will your speech benefit but also your spirit. Your goal is not a sweety sweet, o-ver-ly pre-cise speech; the first effect is saccharine, the second snooty. Instead, you merely need to replace poor vocal habits with good ones. Speech is a learned skill—and learning can be embellished and corrected. A pleasant, well-modulated, easily heard and understood voice projects a positive image of your personality, your character, and your Lord.

Content

A Christian woman should be a lady—not just in her bearing and appearance but in her speech as well. Good grammar is a must for a lady. **Poor grammar reflects not so much a woman's level of education as her level of concern.** Proper grammar doesn't really come from a classroom; it springs from caring how you handle your native language. Poor grammar and slovenly character are automatically connected in the mind of a knowledgeable hearer. In an era when the unsaved consciously or unconsciously express their rebellion against discipline and traditionalism by flouting the rules of grammar, Christians should be doubly careful to *adhere to* those rules! The breakdown of our language is symptomatic of the breakdown of our society; a believer should be the last person in the world guilty of condoning or contributing to that decline. Some people mistakenly feel that bad grammar projects a "folksy" image. But, to put it bluntly in their own jargon, "Them just ain't the folks that really gets to most folks!" **Good grammatical construction, like good manners, is acceptable at every social level; poor grammar severely limits your social mobility—and that in turn limits your effectiveness as a witness for Christ.** Maybe some of you married women say, "'I hardly even get out of the house! About the only people I talk to are my kids!" What do you mean "only"? What greater reason could there be for using good grammar? Your children may learn the *rules* of grammar at school—but they'll learn their *use* of grammar at home. What are you teaching them?

If you have a problem with grammar, do something about it! Towns large and small offer night or mini courses in English for adults. Or go back to your old schoolbooks for concentrated review and practice. If you are still in school, *concentrate* in those English classes. Whatever it takes, do whip your grammar into good shape and keep it that way.

Now think about you vocabulary. Do you use words that are precise, varied, and colorful? Or are you satisfied with tired and inaccurate utterances—"ya know . . . I mean . . . ya know"? Words are fascinating things. Get better acquainted with them. Consult your dictionary often—even on words for which you know the meaning. Don't let advertisers or entertainers influence your vocabulary; too often many in America thoughtlessly parrot these poor sources, creating fads.

Is accurate expression really important? Absolutely. Ask any professional. She'll tell you that the ability to write and speak well plays a key role in attaining success and advancement. A mother or a friend who encourages good vocabulary and grammar usage provides a life gift that's of tremendous value.

Moving on to further consideration of your speech content, I challenge you to record faithfully, for a week, (a) how much you talk and (b) what you talk about. Then at the end of the week, sit down and think seriously about your findings.

Some of the most unlovely contents a born-again woman can have in her speech is gossip—and yet it's prevalent in all our Christian circles. Any one of us who has been the object of gossip knows its hurt:

> The words of a talebearer are as wounds, and they go down into the innermost parts of the belly. **Prov. 18:8**

Yet we persist in gossiping—sometimes even doing so under the guise of presenting prayer requests! Far too many girls and women spread "Have you heards" and "Did you knows" left and right like feathers from a torn pillow.

If a tale-bearing tongue is characteristic of you, consider how Scripture handles the subject. Dwell, for instance, on the interesting company in which God places the loose-tongued person:

> But let none of you suffer as a murderer, or as a thief, or as an evildoer, or as a busybody in other men's matters. **I Pet. 4:15**

It's virtually impossible to come out of such a Bible study without the Holy Spirit's conviction at work on your heart—then you should go to work on your jaw.

Look again at your content/quantity chart. What is the predominant *mood* of your speech? Gloom and doom? Griping? Criticism? Argumentativeness? All of those are unattractive and undesirable in a Christian *because they indicate heart mood* ("*For out of the abundance of the heart the mouth speaketh,*" Matt. 12:34). This powerful truth should drive us to our knees and to our Bibles. The Word will quickly show what our heavenly Father thinks about our speech. For example, how can we cast gloom abroad with our lips when we're told to *"rejoice evermore"* (I Thess. 5:16)? And *Do all things without murmurings and disputings* (Phil. 2:14) immediately wipes out both griping and argumentativeness. In condemning criticism, Scripture accurately applies the descriptive word "backbiting."

Having had Scripture artillery pounding away at the negative moods of our speech, we need to ask the Lord to replace them with their spiritual opposites:

- optimism to replace gloom
- rejoicing to replace griping
- longsuffering and a charitable spirit to replace criticism
- submission to replace argumentativeness.

Take another look at your speech-study chart. What are the *subjects* of your conversations? Soap opera developments? Lurid stories from magazines and newspapers? The lives of movie stars? If so, you are violating the scriptural injunction to think on beautiful, wholesome things. (Remember Philippians 4:8?)

God warns us about negative speech contents as indicators of heart defilement:

> But those things which proceed out of the mouth come forth from the heart; and they defile the man. **Matt. 15:18**

Each one of us should keep a constant check on our tongue. It can be the source of great trouble for us and for others:

> And the tongue is a fire, a world of iniquity: so is the tongue among our members, that it defileth the whole body, and setteth on fire the course of nature; and it is set on fire of hell. **James 3:6**

Efforts to keep our tongue free of offensive utterance can be successful only when we focus on what it says about our heart and upon the fact that God hears—and will judge—every idle word. Jesus Christ warned,

> But I say unto you, That every idle word that men shall speak, they shall give account thereof in the day of judgment. For by thy words thou shalt be justified, and by thy words thou shalt be condemned. **Matt. 12:36–37**

Unattractive speech contents signal the need for reworking of *intake*. Are you willing to submit your enjoyable, habitual "entertainment" sources to God's cleanup? Garbage allowed into the mind produces garbage flowing from the mouth.

Conversation

Having thought about your individual speech, let's now concentrate upon its social aspects. How are your *conversational* skills? It takes more than just an open mouth to make a good conversationalist. Your talking with others is important because you create impressions in them and you reveal yourself.

Good conversation is like a ball game; the ball is supposed to bounce back and forth freely among all members of a group.

Hogging the Ball

Talking too much. This is the number one guarantee for being a bore. What makes you think your comment needs to be made? Every topic that surfaces doesn't require your input. That joke can stay untold. Your opinion doesn't really matter. Have you ever noticed that the Bible itself warns against talking too much?

> In the multitude of words there wanteth not sin: but he that refraineth his lips is wise. **Prov. 10:19**

> A fool hath no delight in understanding, but that his heart may discover [express] itself. **Prov. 18:2**

Bragging. What an unbecoming speech habit for a Christian! Single women boast of their romantic, professional, or scholastic achievements. Married women brag about their children or grandchildren: the sweetest, smartest, best-mannered, most original, most spiritual, beautiful, successful, blah, blah, blah. . . . Ugh!

Including unnecessary details. It takes some people ten minutes to tell you how they crossed Main Street yesterday—because in the process they have to explain the manner of their birth, the weather conditions, the various circumstances that brought them to Main Street, the life history of Great Uncle Henry who lives on that street, and so forth.

Dropping names. The person who inserts such lines as "When I was with Senator Smith last week . . ." or "Yesterday when I was eating with Dr. Important . . ." is a little person trying to enlarge her own image. It fools no one; it's simply tiresome.

Talking only within the confines of your own small world. A mention of husband and children is fine—but don't dump truckloads of information about them every time we meet! All of us need to expand our mental horizons through reading, travel, and so forth in order to extend our "conversational comfort zone."

Dwelling on the past. Some people respond to a simple "How are you today?" with a blow-by-blow harking back to their beginnings!

You never win the game by hogging the conversational ball. You do, however, win a title: ***bore.***

Refusing the Ball

For some girls and women reading this book, the problem is *hiding from* the conversational ball, not hogging it. But consider for a moment—neither one makes for much of a ball game! "I'm so timid," you say with a sigh. Timidity afflicts many of us, and it most often springs from personal insecurity or fear of what people will think of us. We duck mentally whenever the conversational ball heads our way, terrified lest we utter a comment or question to reveal our imagined faults and foibles.

For every socially timid person reading this chapter, I want to include a few special words: Go again to Psalm 139; let your heart listen intently to those blessed words that sing the message of your *security* as a loved one of the Lord. Ask God to give you a firm mental and emotional grip on the picture *He* paints of you in those verses. Go from there to the first chapter of Jeremiah, where the prophet is protesting that he can't speak. God says in verse 8, "Be not afraid of their faces. . . ."

Having accepted encouragement and challenge from the Word, rework your concept of social situations; they are not dreadful, nerve-straining occasions holding ghastly threats for you. They are rich opportunities to meet new friends, to enjoy the interchange of ideas, to bask in the warmth of human companionship and Christian fellowship. And determine that you will *be friendly.* (Proverbs 18:24 reminds us, *A man that hath friends must shew himself friendly.*) People may have judged you to be cold or aloof because of your timidity. There is no way for them to adjust that misconception unless you're willing to come out from behind the walls of protective silence.

Eye Contact

Whether talking with an individual or a group, *eye contact* is important. Don't look at the other person's hair, her left ear, her mouth, or over her shoulder—look her in the eye! Avoiding eye contact gives the impression that you have something to hide and it indicates weak character. When you're talking to a group of people, take each of them into your eye contact; doing so includes them all in the focus of your attention, giving no one a left-out feeling.

Propriety

A believer's conversation should always observe standards of that which is proper. Open discussion of any and all subjects is the order of the day among the unsaved—but for Christian women there are things that should not be discussed in mixed groups, and there are some matters that are inappropriate for open discussion—any time, any place—*period!* This is part of what the Bible calls being "discreet" (Titus 2:5). And of course no one who calls herself a lady should ever be guilty of using crude words and expressions.

The lips of the righteous know what is acceptable: but the mouth of the wicked speaketh frowardness. **Prov. 10:32**

Listening

Do, by all means, develop the ability to listen! Be genuinely interested in other people and in what they have to say. Learning to listen puts the emphasis where it ought to be in conversation—on others rather than on yourself. A good listener is a good conversationalist.

Graciousness and Tact

There are four "sweeteners" all of us need to insert frequently into our speech (*first* of all in our homes!): "Please," "Thank you," "Pardon me," and "I'm sorry." What a world of difference they can make in our daily contacts! Don't you react more pleasurably and compliantly to someone who is polite rather than brusque?

As a final consideration in the matter of conversation, all our social contacts should be marked by *tactfulness.* Tact has been defined as "the delicate perception of the right thing to say or do *without offending.*" An offense is a hurt. Therefore, tactlessness is actually cruelty; how can that be rightly characteristic of Christianity? The only offense we are ever to give is that of the cross—not of our own crassness! We've all experienced the piercing wound made by an inconsiderate remark or question. Tactfulness avoids giving such a wound. Following are a few examples of instances wherein tact needs to be employed.

Don't say, "I know your face, but I just can't remember your name." That says, in essence, "Sorry, Dearie, but you really weren't worth remembering." Instead, say simply, "I'm very sorry but I've forgotten your name."

Don't ask questions that infringe upon a person's privacy. Women are especially liable to offend in this because of feminine curiosity. If a person volunteers information concerning something that is a part of her private life, that's her business. But never probe.

Don't talk about subjects that might bring pain to another. A workable maxim is "Never talk of ropes to a man whose father has been hanged."

Don't comment to one person in a group of fifteen women, "Oh, I just love that dress; you look perfectly beautiful!" It makes all the others feel dowdy.

Don't talk about a social function that only some of the group attended (or plans to attend). That's painful to those not invited.

Don't ask questions or make comments about a person that injure his feelings. In other words, don't be the type who makes "cute" remarks such as, "Well, well—didn't get enough oatmeal as a child, did you, shrimp?"

Or, "Oh, with the size of those ears, you'd better avoid strong winds or you'll fly." Such comments aren't clever; they're cruel.

Don't answer a direct question in such a way as to wound the questioner. For instance, a dear little old lady comes up to you at a church supper and asks, "How did you like my pie?" It was awful; but to be bluntly—and cruelly—truthful would deeply injure the lady's heart. As a Christian you must not lie. The situation can be salvaged, however, with nonspecific words like "interesting," "different," or "unique"—then move on to a sincere compliment for something about the person or thing, such as " . . . and what I always enjoy so much about your pies is how *pretty* they are!"

One final reminder—you are not the important person in Christian conversation; the *other person* is. Articulate the Golden Rule in heart, mind, and mouth.

The Christian woman's avoiding offense in conversation is *not* to be carried into the realm of cowardice. In other words, while we realize we should not offend personally, we must simultaneously remember to faithfully bear testimony—and *the gospel will bring offense.* There must never be spiritual compromise in conversation; that denies the Lord who bought us! The scriptural injunction is

> *Let your speech be alway with grace, seasoned with salt, that ye may know how ye ought to answer every man.* **Col. 4:6**

The "grace" is compassionate consideration; the "salt" loyalty to and proclamation of God's Word.

The woman who exercises her Christian principles in conversation will not only be remembered as a charming person; she will also be enriched herself as she reaches out through the tool of conversation to gain knowledge and understanding of others.

Spiritual X-Rays

*Take heed to yourselves, that your heart be not deceived, and ye turn aside,
and serve other gods, and worship them.*

The Bible makes it painfully clear that our tongue needs constant attention—not only because it's so hard to control but also because it reveals
our mind and heart.

Our modern age is seeing to it that we are surrounded and bombarded
by the sewage of ungodliness. The main purveyors of the corruption are
the entertainment industry and the communications media. But the presence of garbage doesn't equate with the consumption of it; that's a personal choice. Each of us needs to be brought sharply back to awareness that
though humans learn of our heart through our tongue, God constantly
monitors the heart itself. He knows moment by moment what we're allowing to enter and take root there.

Our human conversations will take on the proper characteristics only
as we are faithful in maintaining the lines of communication with our
Lord. Heeding the instructions, confessing and repenting of our weaknesses, and seeking to honor Him provide the vital message to our own
core that controls and shapes our verbal expression.

God has recently zeroed in on me with a potent Scripture passage having to do with speech:

I will speak of the glorious honour of thy majesty, and of thy wondrous works.
Ps. 145:5

O that each of us Christian women might faithfully and consistently use
that to monitor every aspect of our communication.

Generation Considerations

Teens

*Let no man despise thy youth; but be thou an example of the believers, in
word, in conversation, in charity, in spirit, in faith, in purity.*

Even while you're young, people all around you will be listening to your speech, be affected by it, and recognize through it something of the real you. Being aware of that fact may help you discipline your tongue. But your silent times spent in God's Word each day will be the real key; only as you let the Bible do its work internally can your speech rightly represent and please your heavenly Father. To that end, each of us should constantly echo the psalmist's prayer,

Set a watch, O Lord, before my mouth: keep the door of my lips. **Ps. 141:3**

This petition for God's watchfulness will save untold hurt inflicted upon others and harm done to our testimony via our tongue.

Mothers

That our daughters may be as cornerstones, polished after the similitude of a palace.

Please, please don't be a parent who "goes soft" because she wants her daughter to like her and to be her friend! Being used by God to build a cornerstone daughter demands firm, prayerful, consistent *parenting*. Listen constantly and carefully to your daughter's speech, hear her heart in it, and work with the Word to mold her heart to godliness and her lips to guardedness.

Too, your own mouth's ministry is crucial. One of the most personally convicting verses for me in God's description of the virtuous woman of Proverbs 31 is verse 26: "*She openeth her mouth with wisdom; and in her tongue is the law of kindness.*" What a wonderful heritage to provide your daughter.

Mentors

Shewing to the generation to come the praises of the Lord, and his strength, and his wonderful works that he hath done.

Do "come alongside" members of the younger generations. Offer your ear and your heart. Talk to them, yes, but also talk to the Lord for them. May sympathy and compassion sweep through you as you recognize modernity's spiritual battering they experience daily. Listen for their heart needs behind their oral utterances. And in responding to those sensed needs, make Psalm 51:15 your prayer and goal for your own speech: "O Lord, open thou my lips; and my mouth shall shew forth thy praise."

Caution Lights

Take heed therefore that the light which is in thee be not darkness.

Proper speech for a Christian is not self-consciously "spiritual." It's not heavily laced with somber tones, filled with empty platitudes, or bulging with weighty warnings. The world's darkness is filled with disappointment, gloom, and misery. The Christian's life and speech should be characterized by the light of joyfulness. The believer who is too serious, too solemn, is no pattern of godliness; he or she has a problem of joylessness.

All the days of the afflicted are evil: but he that is of a merry heart hath a continual feast. **Prov. 15:15**

Our communication should share that feast. In chapter 28 of Deuteronomy, God through Moses warned His people of the dire results of disobeying His voice. In verse 47 He focuses on their spirit as contributing to that coming punishment:

Because thou servedst not the Lord thy God with joyfulness, and with gladness of heart, for the abundance of all things.

CHAPTER NINE

Etiquette's Spectrum

CHAPTER NINE

Etiquette's Spectrum

Whether therefore ye eat, or drink, or whatsoever ye do, do all to the glory of God. Give none offence, neither to the Jews, nor to the Gentiles, nor to the church of God. **I Cor. 10:31–32**

There be many that say, Who will show us any good? Lord, lift thou up the light of thy countenance upon us. **Ps. 4:6**

"She has beautiful manners." That statement, heard long ago from an older friend, has always intrigued me, and over the years I've come to appreciate both its direct commendation and its indirect comment on character.

Everyone has manners—but they range from abominable to admirable. What makes the difference in the quality of mannerly conduct?

The formal term for mannerliness is etiquette. But what, exactly, does the term mean? A good definition of etiquette is "correct conduct under all circumstances of life." *All* circumstances of life. Genuine mannerliness, then, is not a self-conscious, put-on or taken-off behavior standard. Its core is an integrated part of a person's being. The core itself is simple: *consideration for other people.*

Jesus Christ presented challenging principles for those who have new life in Him. Among them was this:

And as ye would that men should do to you, do ye also to them likewise. **Luke 6:31**

While this is commonly known as the Golden Rule, its practice is not common. It runs contrary to humanity's sinful grain. By nature we want to *take* from everyone around us: kindness, attention, deference . . . But Jesus tells us to turn that natural yearning on its head and to be a *giver* of those things that please us. So it is that the Golden Rule is—like gold— extremely rare. Yet, like gold, its use provides incalculable enrichment. It would be wonderful if we Christians lived out the Golden Rule on a daily basis and observed its lack only among the unsaved. But that is far from reality. The sad fact is that in many cases unregenerate people bring more of etiquette's gold into social intercourse than Christians do. Why?

My husband's grandfather, Dr. Bob Jones Sr., said "You do what you do because you are what you are." Since good manners are a demonstration of thoughtfulness, poor manners indicate unfeeling self-centeredness. What an ugly revelation, and how wholly unlike our Savior! In one of the all-time classics dealing with etiquette, the author pointed to I Corinthians 13 as the ultimate standard for manners. That writer, who never gave the slightest indication of being a born-again woman, nevertheless recognized Scripture to be etiquette's fountainhead. That should make every Christian boor deeply ashamed.

Surely for anyone who has been a Christian for any length of time, I Corinthians 13 is one of the most familiar passages of any in the Bible. Yet its very familiarity can provide an excuse for skim-the-surface, ho-hum reading and response. So before moving on to discuss some dos and don'ts of etiquette, let's settle in at this fountainhead of mannerliness— and of all effective Christian living—and let its waters do a genuine, deep, and personal cleansing. Don't just read the words. Respond in honesty and humility to their scouring power.

> *Though I speak with the tongues of men and of angels, and have not charity, I am become as sounding brass, or a tinkling cymbal.* **13:1**

Consider your mouth. Do you happen to be eloquent? Are you bold and constant in giving a spoken testimony to unsaved people? Do you teach a Bible study? A Sunday school class? Is "Praise the Lord!" often on your lips? None of that counts for a thing if there is not charity (Christlike love) moving your tongue.

And though I have the gift of prophecy, and understand all mysteries, and all knowledge; and though I have all faith, so that I could remove mountains, and have not charity, I am nothing. 13:2

Check your brain, your intellectual abilities, your exercises of spiritual faith. If all of those do not spring from Christlike love, you're a zero, a circle with the ring rubbed out.

And though I bestow all my goods to feed the poor, and though I give my body to be burned, and have not charity, it profiteth me nothing. 13:3

Examine your deeds, your actions, your overall life testimony. Unless those demonstrate and are motivated by Christlike love, God's great hand erases them from the slate of meaning.

I can never read through even those first three verses of the chapter without having my heart smitten with conviction as I am reminded how little of that demanded charity core I possess. And then, of course, the chapter goes on to give specific characteristics of Christlike love as they should be demonstrated daily in our lives. After reading to the end of the list, my heart is unfailingly rebuked. **With so little charity within us, it's no wonder there's so little of good manners in our behavior!**

In undertaking a manners-polishing program, you can encourage yourself by a reminder that *everyone* must learn manners; they are not inborn. Self-centeredness is a human trait evident from early babyhood: we have to *learn* to think of others. Learning etiquette will require two things of you: personal effort and outwardly directed concern.

But, you may argue, why should I adopt an etiquette-improvement program? Think for a moment—we are all social creatures; we don't live as hermits. Social life at every level puts demands upon us that expose our life-guiding principles. There are three outstanding reasons for making etiquette a part of you.

First and most important of all, etiquette is important **to your testimony.** Proper social conduct is a demonstration of the scriptural principles of (a) loving others, (b) living an example, and (c) letting Christ be seen through you. Your manners count for or *against* your Savior. If an unsaved person is nauseated by your table manners, don't think for a moment he's going to be interested in the faith you claim to represent!

Second, etiquette is vitally important **to the comfort and enjoyment of others.** If your manners are uncouth, the people around you are going to be offended, even revolted. If your manners are passable but you're tense from trying to maintain rigid "company behavior," the company is going to sense that tension and in turn be made uneasy.

Third, etiquette is important *for your own self-confidence and ease.* Few circumstances are more uncomfortable than being in a social situation where you're unsure of proper conduct. A good grasp of etiquette, therefore, can eliminate considerable wear and tear on your worry system.

A good verse to memorize in connection with etiquette is I Peter 2:9.

But ye are a chosen generation, a royal priesthood, an holy nation, a peculiar people; that ye should shew forth the praises of him who hath called you out of darkness into his marvellous light.

Notice that phrase "shew forth"—not just "talk forth"! That means your *conduct* is to be a testimony. We who know Christ as Savior are children of the King of heaven—as such, we haven't any excuse for slovenly conduct.

A final few reminders before getting into some etiquette specifics. Good manners depend not so much on the rules as on the reasons behind the rules. Common sense, too, plays an important role in social behavior. That's a handy thought to fall back on when you don't know specifically what to do in a situation; ask yourself what action would *common sense* plus *consideration* prescribe? It is also important to remember that *the lady always sets the standard!* Do you resent the sloppy manners of your boyfriend or husband? Check on your own conduct. Someone has well said that a lady is a woman who lets a man enjoy being a gentleman.

Guy–Girl Etiquette

Because we've mentioned the standard-setting responsibility of women, and because many who read this book will be in what might be called "the age of becoming," it's appropriate to spend time discussing guy-girl relationships. The world's ungodliness has greatly darkened our Christian premarital landscape.

This topic best fits the present format as a part of etiquette due to the broad definition presented in the opening of the chapter: "correct conduct under all circumstances of life." There is desperate need for Christian young people to return to *biblically correct conduct* in guy-girl relationships. Because propriety has been thrown aside, our young people are only a half step behind America's pagan teenagers in shattered purity, sexually transmitted diseases, illegitimate pregnancies, and tragic marriages.

Hebrews 13:4 reads, *"Marriage is honourable in all, and the bed undefiled: but whoremongers and adulterers God will judge."*

God created men and women to be attracted to each other. That natural attraction becomes clearly active during puberty as the body transitions into its mature functioning. An individual must correctly and constantly monitor that magnetism in order to obey God's plan for maintaining physical purity until marriage. As stated earlier, the lady's spirit and behavior are strategic throughout every area of etiquette. That principle must operate strongly as teens move into the pairing-off years. A girl's teasing, flirting, and suggestive talk may seem innocent fun to her. But to a teenage boy they can present mental and physical temptation. Girls, *recognize the immensity of your responsibility* to monitor God-pleasing relationships. When there is mutual respect, social enjoyment, and lighthearted companionship due to relational etiquette, young people can experience the teen years as uniquely wonderful. Keeping such relationships in the realm of casually enjoyable friendship takes pressure off both genders. The two general components of successful monitoring are attitudes and actions.

Attitudes. Some mindsets predispose a girl to trouble in boy-girl relationships. One of those is described by the term "boy crazy." If a teenage girl centers too much thought too soon and too often upon boys, she makes herself vulnerable. The Bible urges each of us to wisdom, and it counsels against foolishness. A girl does well to heed Scripture, keeping herself from mental and emotional fluff. Boys respond to a boy-crazy girl in one of two ways: with scornful dislike and disregard or with the intention to take advantage of her. Girls, keep your attitude toward guys casual. Focus your emotional attention on safer objects—sports, horses, or hobbies. As you move through the years from early to late teens, don't let your attitude become "I have to find a man" or "If I don't get married, I can never be happy." Such thoughts blatantly oppose the Bible's pronouncement, *"Ye are complete in him [Jesus Christ]"* (Col. 2:10). Too, they weaken your defenses against Satan's efforts to sidetrack or destroy you.

A second attitude to cultivate as a teen is respect and appreciation for your mother and father. Even if you have unsaved parents, recognize that their love and wisdom are God's gift to you and they form a wonderful wall of protection. Don't breach that wall by disregard or disobedience. Proverbs 30:17 should send warning chills down your spine:

> The eye that mocketh at his father, and despiseth to obey his mother, the ravens of the valley shall pick it out, and the young eagles shall eat it.

Actions. Unwise actions in guy-girl relationships are many, but I'll deal with just a few. First, aggressiveness. Too many Christian young women have unknowingly absorbed the "strong, sexy, and savvy" spirit of unsaved womanhood. Nowhere does the Bible commend a woman who barges her way through life seeking attention, leadership, or marriage. When God gives a woman prominence, she's honored—as was Deborah. But when she pursues it personally, she is chastised—as was Miriam.

In guy-girl relationships a Christian girl is wrongly aggressive when she asks or hints for a date, when she flirts, when she plots to be where a guy will "happen" to cross her path, when she dresses, talks, or behaves suggestively, and when she takes the initiative to call a guy on the telephone, write notes, or send him unsolicited e-mails. Realize that a girl's aggressiveness is counterproductive because guys want to be the aggressors; it's part of their makeup. If some of the statements warning you against being forward seem archaic, it's because your mind has been corrupted *"through philosophy and vain deceit, after the tradition of men, after the rudiments of the world, and not after Christ"* (Col. 2:8).

Your behavior when with a guy or group of guys should demonstrate propriety. Don't let lighthearted fun deteriorate into undisciplined romping with squeals, loudness, or rampaging. Do think of guys as friends, and enjoy being with them in casual settings. At the same time, however, remember to consider other people, and be aware of how your behavior may negatively affect or even offend them. Continually ask yourself, "What is my *Christian testimony* right now, both in the eyes of the friends I'm with and in the eyes of the public looking on?"

Never trust your flesh; it's pitifully weak. Carefully guard yourself against settings and circumstances that spell danger in relationships. Consider cars as vehicles to move you from one place to another—not as private compartments in which to talk overlong, sit too close to each other, or get into kissing and petting. Do not *ever* let a guy into your home when your parents are not there. Beware of double dates in which the other couple is into heavy physical contact. Analyze each togetherness occasion ahead of time for whatever potential opportunity for temptation it may hold. It's far better to refuse an invitation—no matter how flattering or exciting—than to regret it forever after.

A prudent man foreseeth the evil, and hideth himself; but the simple pass on, and are punished. **Prov. 27:12**

Although new texts have been written and are helpful for technological etiquette and so forth, the old standard books are still supreme: specifically, the extensive works of Amy Vanderbilt and Emily Post. I read a small stack of recent etiquette books; though upbeat, the "modernized" moral tone becomes offensive, as does some language usage. The core concepts have not been improved upon.

Invitations

The rule for invitations is extremely simple: *respond* to an invitation right away. Your host or hostess needs to "count heads" in order to plan food and other details involved in the occasion. If the invitation is issued in person or by telephone rather than in written form, and you're unable to answer immediately, say so—and then get back as soon as possible either to decline or accept.

An invitation extends *only* to those whose names are written on it or are mentioned verbally. Never show up with an extra someone you decided to take along—including children.

Once you've accepted an invitation, keep the commitment. Only genuine illness, accident, or other major setback qualifies as an excuse—and in such a case you must call as early as possible to let your host(s) know you'll be unable to come. Anytime you don't attend a function to which you've committed, your failure says, "It just isn't worth my time and effort." What a slap in the face for a host or hostess!

General Behavior as a Guest

When you go as guest to someone's home, it's a nice gesture to take a thoughtful hostess gift. The purpose, type, and length of your visit should determine the nature and expense of your gift.

Proper behavior as a guest is based upon remembering that you are not in your own home—every area, item, decision, and so forth is the property or prerogative of your host or hostess.

Contain your curiosity. Do not ask to see any thing or place the hostess does not offer for your observation. If you absolutely must excuse yourself for a trip to the bathroom, don't use your time therein to snoop through cabinets.

My own horrifying experiences as a hostess all center upon the annual Senior Picnic here at Bob Jones University. The University provides a splendid fried chicken picnic meal each fall for all of our graduating seniors. That means we serve anywhere from eight hundred to a thousand people during the evening. The main course is served on our back lawn, but dessert is served in our home so the students can feel they've had an opportunity to "be at home" with our family. The phrase is acted out to surprising extremes. Students open and look in our closets. They examine drawers and cabinets. They look under our beds. They get into our tub or shower (with their shoes on) and have snapshots taken. They sit and bounce on our beds. Yes, these are college seniors looking forward to receiving their undergraduate degrees in just a few months! That kind of kindergarten-age behavior certainly doesn't advertise positively for their home training or for their personal respect for other people's property. Sadly, I hear from friends that adults well along the road of life perform with similar lack of manners in the homes they visit.

Table Etiquette

This is a subject calling for extensive detailing. It's really impossible to overemphasize the importance of table manners. When large corporations consider hiring or promoting someone for a responsible position, executives will take that person and his wife out for a meal—and watch their conduct at the table. What is seen at the table can either work for or against winning the position—because the person occupying the position will represent the company. *How much weightier is our representation of our Savior and Lord!*

In the following discussion, only a very few items can be covered. I would urge you to brush up on the subject of etiquette by reading a complete book on the subject. In this chapter, I can touch only on items that seem to loom largest in necessity and practicality.

Seating

As a lady, wait for the gentleman's assistance in seating you. If he is not immediately attentive to the task, simply stand quietly. There are always occasions when each man at the table has more than one woman to assist. Don't feel awkward waiting your turn, and don't glare or dart glances of "Hurry up, for pity's sake!" There is a commonsense exception: if the men are significantly outnumbered at the table and your place is several women away from one of the overworked gentlemen, go ahead and seat yourself.

When the man approaches to help you, step to the side of the chair opposite the direction of his approach. That is, if he comes from your left, step to the right of your chair. You have thus cleared the way for him to pull the chair away from the table. Then, slip into the chair from the side to which you've moved.

Remember that the gentleman is going to move the chair (and you) toward the table. So don't descend onto the chair with all your weight. Take your seat, then use your thigh muscles to lift your own weight partially as he scoots the chair forward. If the poor man has to heave you and the chair closer to the table, he's courting back strain! Sit down gracefully, establish good posture, and maintain it throughout the meal.

Napkins

Place your dinner napkin, half-open, in your lap. (In just-dessert situations, a smaller dessert napkin should be fully opened.) Remember that a napkin is meant to be a *lap*kin. It shouldn't be tucked into a collar or draped over a stomach bulge. It's to be used for fingers and mouth—not for your nose. The ultimate way to sicken table companions is to blow your nose on a napkin. Think ahead; always take a handkerchief or tissue to the table with you. If you absolutely must blow your nose, excuse yourself from the table and go into another room to do so.

Serving and Passing

Food moves *toward the right* around the table. (The only exception is when someone asks for a particular dish and it is much closer to pass it to the left rather than to the right.) There is a proper way to receive and pass food in its trip around the table:

- receive dish or platter with your *right* hand (crossing your body with that arm),
- transfer serving piece to your *left* hand for holding while you serve yourself, and
- pass the food to the person on your right with your *left* hand (again, crossing your body with your arm in the process). This method of receiving and passing has been universally adopted because it is the most considerate of those sitting to either side of you since it reduces the possibility of your hitting them with an elbow or arm. Also, by giving you greater strength and control than a "backhand" pass, it helps you to avoid spills.

In serving yourself, take only enough food for a moderate-sized helping. Consider the hunger pangs of the rest of the people at the table!

Always use the serving utensil provided—never your own fork or spoon—to take the food from the serving vessel. Nobody wants your germs or food bits!

Never take food from a platter or bowl without taking the serving vessel. Haven't you responded, say, to a request for the rolls—then had the asker take a roll and leave you holding the platter? Pretty clear expression of thoughtlessness and ingratitude, isn't it?

Don't stop the food's progress around the table. Some people serve themselves, then put the platter or bowl on the table, never considering those farther along who've not yet been served.

If you are a guest at a meal at which the host or hostess serves the plates with food from his or her place at the table, it is proper to indicate your desire for a smaller-than-average portion of a particular food. But if food is served "blue-plate" style, already having food on the plate, do not ask for an adjustment.

Use of Flatware

How do you react when sitting down to a table at which various sizes and shapes of flatware appear on both sides of the plates? With dread as you realize you don't know what utensil to use for which food? With panic and self-consciousness? Those negative reactions can be laid to rest by the knowledge of two simple principles: (a) use silver working from *the outside in* toward the plate, and (b) watch the hostess for cues. Study this diagram to see the outside-in principle.

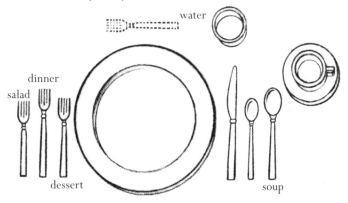

Inevitably, there will be times when you're unsure how a particular food is to be eaten. In such instances, unobtrusively watch your hostess.

Many people don't know how to wield the silver once they decide which piece is proper. The most-often-broken rule of correct usage comes with an ordinary knife and fork.

Incorrect silver usage gives offense—no matter how artfully your pinkie may be curled! Perhaps the very harshness of that statement is needed to awaken you to your responsibility: consider—and relearn, if need be—the proper handling of a knife and fork.

A fork should be neither a dagger (a) nor a shovel (b).

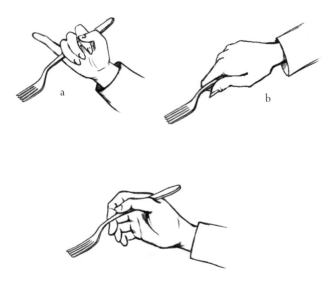

The proper way to hold a fork or spoon

Use the *only* correct method for cutting.

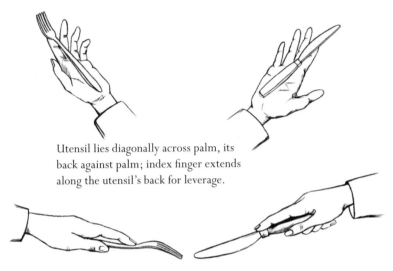

Utensil lies diagonally across palm, its
back against palm; index finger extends
along the utensil's back for leverage.

Fork tines are placed in the portion that will become your
bite; the knife cuts on the far side of the fork's position.
Note: Those who are left-handed will simply reverse hands,
but use the identical positions and techniques.

If you have never had the opportunity to learn the proper handling of
a knife and fork, *learn it now and make it habitual.* Few changes of behavior have such power to add cultural polish to your social image. And few
things incorrectly done more joltingly mark you as uncultured.

Cut only one piece of food at a time. Starvation will not overtake you
between cutting tasks.

When not using your knife for cutting, it should rest "cornered" across
the plate rim. The handle should *not* rest on the table.

Eating

Don't begin to eat until (a) everyone at the table has been served, or
(b) your hostess puts her fork on her plate, begins eating, or indicates verbally that you should go ahead.

Keep your nonactive hand in your lap while eating, except when you
have to cut, butter bread, steady a dish, and so forth. Don't prop yourself
up while eating or put your elbows on the table.

213

When you're eating at someone's home, do take at least a bit of everything that has been prepared. Your hostess has put hard work into preparing the meal. Don't say, "I don't like that" or "I'm on a diet." The *only* legitimate excuse for refusing a particular food is an allergy to it.

Remember that flatware is for eating—not for *gesturing.* Particles of food can easily be slung from a waving fork or knife.

Once any piece of flatware has been used, it should not be returned to the tabletop; it's put on your plate (or salad plate, saucer, and so forth, according to where the piece is used).

Do *not* wipe off or lick off food from a fork, knife, or spoon as you move from eating one food to another.

It is permissible to cut unwieldy chunks of lettuce, tomato, and other items in your salad. However, you should cut only one bite at a time, not the entire salad.

If you encounter something in a meal that cannot be cut, what should you do? Make a clever comment about "'shoe-leather meat"? Choke it down uncut? Neither. Keep your cutting attempts inconspicuous, and without calling attention to your difficulties, simply leave the stubborn portion on your plate.

Avoid stuffing your mouth—either by taking overlarge bites or by "piggybacking"—adding a bite before having chewed and swallowed a prior bite completely. A stuffed mouth is grossly unattractive. But, don't go to the other extreme of "itty bitty" bites whereby it takes more than one bite to empty a fork. That is not a sign of delicacy or femininity—only of silliness. The rule is to take a moderate amount of food onto your fork or spoon and to empty that utensil in one bite or sip.

Always chew *with your lips closed.* No one wants to see or hear you prepare your food for your stomach!

In eating soup, tip and move the spoon *away* from you. That's to prevent the shovel-it-in look; it also helps avoid drips landing in your lap. It is permissible to tip the cup or bowl to get the last drops of a liquid food— but the vessel should be tipped away from you. Do *not* slurp as you take soup from the spoon.

Never talk with your mouth full. It can spray your table companion with partially chewed food or cause you to choke. Keeping this rule in mind, avoid asking someone else a question while his or her mouth is full. If someone should ask you a question while you're chewing, silently indicate (napkin-to-lips gesture, for example) that you need a moment before you can reply.

Cut and manage your food neatly. By all means, don't premix it on your plate. Sure, everyone knows it will eventually get mixed; but let the blending take place in the out-of-sight location the Lord intended!

What about dealing with something in your mouth that's unchewable? You certainly shouldn't attempt to swallow the offending piece whole. "Cafe coronary" (choking to death) can result from that unwise decision. Instead, wait until conversation attention is focused elsewhere, then unobtrusively (behind your napkin) remove the offending portion from your mouth and return it to the plate. Also, hide the unsightly discarded piece as much as possible among other leftovers on your plate, as well. Do not call attention to your chewing difficulties.

There are several foods that are a special challenge to eat. Perhaps foremost among them is spaghetti. Delicious as it is, nearly every bite results in dangling, awkward, spattering strands. Of course, you can surrender to the difficulty by cutting the spaghetti into fork-sized lengths (one bite at a time). But that's considered cowardly. There is, however, a method for eating spaghetti that's as neat as possible. It is a two-handed approach: hold the fork in your right hand (for left-handedness, just reverse the whole description); your left hand holds a large-bowled spoon. Take a few strands of spaghetti onto your fork, then place the ends of the fork tines in the spoon and turn the fork over and over so that the spaghetti is rolled around the fork tines. When most of the strands have been captured, take the bite to your mouth. Almost inevitably there will be one or two danglers, but they will be far fewer than in other methods.

Small, manageable pieces of fried chicken are considered finger food—drumstick, thigh, or wing. However, an oversized piece—a breast or quarter portion—should be eaten with a fork. If the hostess is using knife and fork on smaller pieces of the chicken, however, you as a guest are obliged to do so too.

Then there are olives with pits intact. How to eat them gracefully? Take the whole olive into your mouth and eat the meat from the seed. Then move the seed to the very front of your mouth (lips closed, tongue doing the moving work); finally, using thumb and forefinger, remove the pit and place it to one side on your plate.

Finishing a Meal

When you have completed your meal, place knife, fork, and spoon across the middle or upper half of your plate, with handles parallel to the table's edge. A seafood fork would also be placed across the dinner plate, unless the fish course has been removed earlier. A soup spoon may be left in the soup bowl or on its service plate, and a salad fork and butter knife on their respective plates.

Don't bother to refold your napkin neatly. Just leave it beside your plate crumpled or lightly folded.

Once the meal is finished, elbows may rest on the table in order to facilitate conversation.

Social Etiquette

All of your proper social conduct is based upon an important rule of behavior: *A lady never calls attention to herself by loudness of dress, voice, or behavior.*

Social Grace

Social grace is *the ability to appear comfortably at ease in any situation,* and its vital component is poise. People with poise apply a tripartite formula: quietness + control + concentration on others. Let's consider each one.

Quietness. Replace fidgeting, nervous mannerisms, and too-loud or too-abundant talking with quietness. Physical or vocal loudness reveals that you're ill at ease; quietness says poise.

Control. The pressure of social occasions brings out negative personality traits: the timid person withdraws more than ever, whereas the extrovert becomes obnoxious and overbearing. To avoid both extremes, and to contribute positively to the occasion, recognize your own tendency, and exercise self-control.

Concentration on others. This is the real key to social ease. The more time you think about yourself, the more miserable you'll be. Instead, look around the room for someone who obviously is not a part of any conversational group; go to that person, introduce yourself, and initiate a conversation; concentrate on making your new acquaintance happy to be there. Spend the entire occasion repeating that practice, and your efforts to help others feel comfortable will help you feel comfortable as well.

Social Occasions and the Clock

Forgetting time's passage makes things hard on others—namely, your host and hostess. At the end of every company occasion there is clean-up work waiting. Your staying time for a meal should be limited to two hours, and for a drop-in one hour. It's much better to bid farewell to hosts who wish you could stay than to stay and have them wish you'd leave! And once you start to go, do so! Don't stand lingering over good-byes.

Withdraw thy foot from thy neighbour's house; lest he be weary of thee, and so hate thee. **Prov. 25:17**

It is proper to offer clean-up help to your hostess. If she declines, do *not* insist.

Social Occasions and Conversation

A social occasion is meant to be a time of relaxation and enjoyment as people take the opportunity to visit with one another. The spirit of such a time can be ruined and the attendees wearied by someone who introduces and long-windedly expresses herself on heavy topics. If you need to talk business or detail your personal, family, or ministry problems, *make an appointment.*

Introductions

The simplest way to handle introducing people to each other is with a "name first" technique:

- In introducing a man and a woman, say the *woman's* name first. ("Mrs. Brown, may I introduce Mr. Smith?")
- If two people of the same sex are to be introduced, mention the *older person's* name first. ("Mr. Seventy-five, may I introduce Mr. Fifty?")
- When introducing two women of about the same age, mention the *married woman's* name first. ("Mrs. Green, I'd like you to meet Miss White.")
- The *more prominent person's* name should be spoken first. ("Senator Smith, I'd like you to meet my mother, Mrs. Jones.")
- When someone joins a conversational group, mention the *newcomer's* name first; then proceed around the room or group in an orderly fashion, indicating each person as named (by a gesture, nod of the head, etc.) in order to help the newly arrived person put names with faces.

If you introduce people and then move on, leave them with a conversational aid. For example, you might mention an interest they share, a biographical item of one of them, a note about one's occupation, or *something* to serve as a springboard for their further talk. It's awkward for anyone to be abandoned by an introducer with nothing but names given.

When you approach someone for conversation, *never* say, "Do you remember me?" That's egotistical on your part and embarrassing to the other person. *Don't assume you have been remembered*—give your name and, if necessary, some brief "context" thing to help the person recall who you are and where he or she met you. Conversely, when you can't remember someone's name, just politely ask it.

Meeting, Speaking, and Shaking Hands

When a man and a woman meet, it is the *woman's* place to speak first: that's one instance when a lady's initiative is not brazen. Men almost always shake hands in meeting each other; women seldom do. A woman shows good manners when she offers her hand when introduced to a man. And by all means, ladies, learn to give a *good* handshake! Don't use a bone-crushing "I lift weights, too!" grip, but don't try for ultra-femininity with a limp, slithery, "dead fish" technique. A good handshake has four qualities: it is firm, elbow level, brief, and sincere.

Don't be an "instant buddy." People are increasingly breaking the barrier of respect by immediately using first names. That's an unbecoming characteristic. *Refrain from calling anyone by his or her first name until asked to do so.* The exception, of course, is when dealing with those considerably younger than yourself.

Now let's consider some other places and situations that call for particular rules of behavior.

Restaurants. It's a special treat to go out for dinner to a restaurant. But there are some principles of conduct for such occasions that can enhance your testimony as a polished Christian lady.

Upon entering the restaurant in overcoat weather, the man checks his coat. (When he retrieves the coat(s) after the meal, he should tip the attendant at least $1.) The woman may either have him check hers also, or she may take it to the table. In the latter case, she may either remove the coat while standing and place it on an empty chair at their table or sit first and then remove it, letting it drape over the back of her own chair.

The gentleman tells the hostess or *maitre d'* how many are in your party—so don't speak up when asked, "How many in your party, please?"

If the *maitre d'*, waiter, or waitress leads the way to your table, the woman goes directly behind him or her. However, if there is no one to show you to the table, the gentleman leads the way. The principle at work in this instance is that he is acting protectively toward the lady, "breaking the way" through the room's traffic.

The waiter or *maitre d'* seats the woman or her escort does so. I've seen men plop happily into a chair held out by a waiter, oblivious that the courtesy is being offered to the lady.

If you are carrying a purse or other items, they should be put on the floor, an empty chair, or on your lap—never on the table. This rule definitely applies to baby-carrying devices.

In a fine restaurant the waiter may place the napkin in your lap.

Suppose you and your escort have been seated at a table, served your water, and now sit with menus in hand; all at once you realize that the prices are much higher than you anticipated. Do you make a fuss, exclaiming loudly over "sky-high prices"? Do you bounce out in an obvious huff? Either of those reactions will blacken your testimony. Instead, choose one of two actions: (1) search the menu until you can find a selection within your financial range, or (2) let your escort summon the waiter or waitress and explain in a quiet, mannerly way that you will not be having dinner there after all. You had looked forward to his or her service and so forth, but . . . Then quietly make your exit.

Many really fine restaurants have their menus printed in a foreign language—notably French. *Don't* pretend you know what the dishes are and choose one via the eenie-meenie-minie-mo method. The proper thing to do is for your escort to ask the waiter to describe the various dishes. You will not only be doing the correct thing; you will also bring delight to the person serving you. Waiters at such restaurants take immense pleasure in describing the establishment's culinary delights.

The gentleman suggests two or three possible selections that lie within his price range, and the lady *never* orders beyond the price he has indicated.

The lady tells her escort what she wishes to order, and he delivers the message to the waiter. You need not speak to the person waiting table unless directly addressed. Of course, to respond to a "Do you want butter or sour cream on your potato, ma'am?" by whispering, "Tell her I want butter, George," would be ridiculous.

In some European dining situations, the waiter will approach from your left and serve your plate item by item. He will expect you to indicate when you have received a large enough serving of each food.

When eating in an informal restaurant, the basic rules of etiquette apply, but common sense will dictate necessary adjustments.

If a woman stops by your table to talk, your escort must rise and *remain standing until she moves away.* You do not have to do so unless she is a much older woman. It is never proper, however, for you to continue eating while someone stands at your table talking. Looking at the situation from the reverse angle, realize that a meal must thus halt for politeness' sake, and don't *you* be a table side conversationalist. Consideration for other people will help you remember that restaurants are *eating* places. Extended or noisy socializing disturbs those around you, curbs servers' efficiency, and delays the seating of the customers waiting for your table.

In general, the greatest thoughtfulness in a restaurant situation is simply to greet anyone you might recognize with a smile, nod, and few words, as in "Hello, Jim . . . Carol. Good to see you." But keep moving. You should never call out to someone several tables away or make a noisy meeting scene.

When you're eating in a restaurant without an escort, leave the expected tip for the one who serves you: 15 to 20 percent of the bill. Waiters and waitresses receive low salaries; they depend upon tips. If you make extra work for your server, ask for any kind of special accommodation, or tie up a table overlong, *increase the tip*. Women are notorious for not tipping or for under-tipping. If you are just too stingy to tip, *don't* leave a tract! Far too many true stories are told of Christian testimonies shattered by boorish restaurant behavior, the "after church" crowds that don't tip, and the Christians who ask a blessing over their food but mistreat the server.

Church Behavior

How are your manners in church? Do you leave them at home? It's easy to fall into too-casual conduct that is not only inconsiderate toward others but also irreverent toward God. First of all, recognize that church is a special place and that you go to church primarily as an act of *worship* among other believers. We modern-day Christians need to be impressed anew with the holiness of the God we love and serve! We have picked up a great deal of the world's cheapening, silly attitude that God is "the man upstairs." A new sense of God's holiness will shake us into realizing the beauty and privilege we have of worshiping Him as an act of love. That word "worship" should set our attitude and actions for church conduct: quiet, respectful, and reverent at all times. The circuslike attitudes sometimes displayed in the house of the Lord are entirely out of keeping with worship. Learn also to sit *still* in church services. Those around you can be maddeningly distracted if you are changing positions, crossing and uncrossing your legs, cracking your knuckles, straightening your hair, flipping through your Bible, drumming your fingers on the bench or chair arm. You may think those things insignificant. However, they can so distract attention that the sermon being preached is unheard. As we personally obey God's instruction,

Be still, and know that I am God . . .

we may simultaneously clear the path to blessing or even to salvation for someone else.

Of course, as Christians, the friends who mean the most to us are those in our church family. That is as it should be, and the warmth of friendship and fellowship should be evident when we get together. But the visiting should be conducted *before* and *after* the church services outside the sanctuary.

General Deportment

"Decorum" is a word seldom heard (much less *exhibited!*) in our day. Ideally, however, it should characterize every Christian woman. Decorum is simply *propriety and good taste in behavior.* Propriety demonstrates the principle stated earlier that a lady *never* draws *attention to* herself by loudness of dress, voice, or action. Good taste will avoid inappropriate actions such as scratching your head, picking your nose, touching your teeth, and biting your fingernails in public. Obviously, decorum entails self-discipline and others-focus.

Anonymity

How do you behave when you think you're anonymous? For instance, when you're in a city some distance from your own and you feel no one knows you. Do you drop your restrained behavior like a hot potato? Actually, the way you conduct yourself when you can claim anonymity is a sure mark of what you really are. And, after all, the one you should be seeking to represent and to please above all others is always with you, always seeing, always listening. That's the reason our mannerly behavior must be constant.

Deference

A lady always demonstrates respect for age. Whether the older person is a man or woman, you should rise, hold doors, carry packages, and so forth as occasions present themselves. Nor is age the only reason for deferential behavior. Scripture tells us we're to live "in honour preferring one another."

Masculine Attention

What about gentlemanly assistance? It's great! Accept it—graciously. There are specific situations in which you can expect a man to offer his help. On curbs or stairs he will offer his arm. (Take it lightly—don't throw him off-balance!) Getting on public conveyances, he will let you mount the steps first and will offer his hand to give you balance; getting off, he will lead, then reach up to offer his hand as you descend. Crossing streets he doesn't have to offer his arm except in adverse weather conditions or especially heavy traffic, though he may do so. He will, of course, open doors for you. A revolving door offers him special challenge. He will lean past you, get the door started, then let you enter the first compartment while he enters the next. He will also assist you getting into and out of cars by opening and closing the door for you. And, finally, he will help you get into and out of coats, jackets, and so forth. *Whenever* a man assists you, *thank him*! And that doesn't mean only your favorite tall, dark, handsome escort; it also means the nondescript little stranger who opens the door at the drugstore! A woman who doesn't appreciate gentlemanly conduct doesn't deserve gentlemanly conduct.

Common Discourtesies

More unmannerly actions arise from thoughtlessness than from malice. Such is the case in blocking a doorway or aisle. Whether conversation or action stalls you in such places, think of those whose progress you're impeding, and *get out of the way of traffic* before continuing your business of the moment. Another type of thoughtless behavior is whispering or talking during a church service, concert, or other program. Save your comments until after the occasion. Other people are more interested in seeing and hearing what they came to see and hear than in your bobbing head and running commentary.

How do you behave when standing in lines? Do you exercise patience and good manners, or do you let your impatience make you grumble and shove? Remember that *no one* considers line-standing an interesting sport; and most are in as much of a hurry as you are. Don't add to their misery by your comments, and don't break in line.

Finally, avoid staring and glaring. For instance, if someone inadvertently bumps you in a crowded store aisle, do you dart withering glances toward the offender? Do you stare at conspicuously unfortunate people such as those who are crippled, crying, or very shabbily dressed? Realize, instead, that you can offer them a kindness—by allowing them the dignity of privacy!

Driving Etiquette

One of a man's favorite expressions on a highway or street is "woman driver!" There is never a question about the spirit in which he says it. Actually, women often are better drivers than men. But there are ways to improve one's driving and decrease the exclamations of disgust. *Think* while you drive; tragedy can result from a moment's inattention. Observe speed limits: they're the law of the land. Driving too fast endangers lives; so does driving too slow. Use the left lane for passing—not for dawdling. Finish your makeup, breakfast, and phone calls before you get into the car. Let others merge into your lane of traffic. Signal your turning or lane-changing intentions—others on the road can't guess what you plan to do. Do *not* swing left to make a right turn or right to make a left turn. Don't drift out of your chosen lane.

Public Programs

Arrive on time. Sit still throughout the performance. Don't make whispered or murmured comments. Don't leave until the program has ended. When entering or exiting a row *face toward the stage* and voice your apology as you move along toward your seat. *Turn off cell phone, pager, and alarm watch.* Be sure to have breath mints or cough drops with you to stifle a possible cough.

Letter Writing

Do write letters and notes—don't reduce all of your correspondence to e-mail. Use stationery, not notebook paper or legal pad sheets. The most appropriate stationery is good quality stock in ivory or white. If you like a bit of color, confine it to subtle hues on the page borders and envelope lining. Use only blue or black ink. Don't type personal letters. Be sure to write and mail any thank-you note or letter within one week after the occasion at which you were a guest.

Telephone Manners

Speak clearly and pleasantly when answering the telephone. Don't be irritated or impatient. If the caller asks for someone else, identify yourself, explain that So-and-So is not available, and ask if you can help by taking a message. If you have an answering machine, keep its recorded message brief; don't try to be original or clever.

Cell phones. There are roughly one hundred fifty million cell phones in the United States; they're proving to be great destroyers of courtesy. Control your cell phone usage and demonstrate good manners by giving your time and attention to the people you're with instead of those you might call. Think of your cell phone as a hedge against emergency—not an enablement for all-the-time and anyplace gabbing. In many instances, cell phones are used ostentatiously to demonstrate the owner's importance. If you absolutely must use your cell phone in public, speak quietly and be brief. There are, however, few if any messages that can't be recorded and wait for your answer.

E-mail Etiquette

This marvelous technological invention affords convenience and speed; it also presents new challenges. Do respond to a direct message (not to junk mail or forwards). Indicate your topic on the subject line—it helps your recipient prioritize and frame a prompt answer. Be careful about spelling and grammar. Do *not* use the computer at your workplace for personal correspondence. Use the recipient's name followed by a comma in beginning an e-mail note. Don't type in capital letters; it's considered shouting. Experts warn against ever saying anything in e-mail you wouldn't read aloud in public.

Fax Etiquette

Keep this type of correspondence legible and neat. Make your message clear, brief, and to the point. Remember that it may not be kept private. Do *not* use fax to extend a last-minute invitation for a social event; it may be a quick way to try to cover forgetfulness, but it's nevertheless an insult.

Tipping Etiquette

Restaurants are not the only places tips are expected. In all such establishments, *those who tip badly are regarded with disdain.*

Hotels. Tip at least a dollar per bag to the bellhop (more for very heavy bags). Room service gets 15 percent (check the bill to be sure it hasn't already been added). The maid should receive a couple of dollars per day. The doorman should be given a dollar if he hails a taxi, and more if it's raining. The concierge should be given 10 to 20 percent of the cost of program tickets he procures for you. If he makes your restaurant reservations give him $5–10.

Beauty salons. A tip of 15 to 20 percent is proper for the cosmetologist and a dollar or two for the person who washes your hair. You do not tip the owner or manager.

Transportation. For a taxi or limousine you should tip 10 to 15 percent. A parking valet at a hotel or restaurant receives several dollars. Airport skycaps are given a dollar per bag and more for heavy ones.

Sports Etiquette

When you're a participant in any sport, you of course follow the rules of the game. There are also some etiquette factors to be observed when you're a spectator. Be on time; otherwise, you disturb those who were. Show your tickets to an usher and follow him to your seat. Raise your arm to get the attention of the person selling food, snacks, or drinks—don't yell. Keep your cheering short of exhibitionism. Do not call insults to or about the other team or officials. Remember people are sitting behind you; be aware that if you jump up and down or stand for an extended time you block their view. If someone in front of you blocks the view, it's proper to ask him or her politely to sit down. When moving through pregame or postgame crowds, don't push or make loud, impatient noises.

Professional Etiquette

When a Christian woman works in any professional organization, she must take extra care with regard to her behavior—particularly in man-woman relationships. She has a wonderful opportunity to carry spiritual light into the workplace. But she must also protect herself against the dangers of darkness that are there.

Sexual harassment in the workplace receives a good deal of publicity. Just what that term means may be unclear. In 1994 the Tucson, Arizona, Equal Employment Opportunity Office published a helpful definition:

- unwelcome or unwanted sexual advances
- requests or demands for sexual favors
- other verbal or physical conduct based on gender when this behavior:
  - is a term or condition of employment (explicit or implicit)
  - is used as a basis for advancement decisions
  - unreasonably interferes with work performance or creates an intimidating, hostile, or offensive working environment.

There are some protective rules of conduct between men and women that should be observed in business situations.

- There should be no physical contact other than a handshake.
- When compliments are in order, focus on professional skill and accomplishment—not on appearance.
- Use proper names; avoid any terms of endearment.
- In cases in which criticism or confrontation is needed, focus on the offensive behavior or speech, not on the person.
- Send gifts to a business associate's home only as part of a group—never from you individually.

- Don't let someone get away with offensive behavior. Confront him about the problem behavior or speech, and end with a question that requires a response.
- Don't remain alone in the office after hours with a man. If work requires extended hours, ask a third person to stay with you.

There are also some "genderless" principles for business situations.

- Whoever gets to a door first opens it.
- The person closest to the elevator enters it first.
- Both men and women are expected to rise to greet a client or guest, whether the guest is male or female.
- Shaking hands is without gender; the man needn't wait for the woman to initiate the move.
- If a woman is hosting a business luncheon, she's the one who pays for it.
- Do not take on personal chores for a male coworker (fixing his coffee, replacing a button, etc.).

Language Etiquette

English is increasingly used around the globe. However, foreign accents can make our language difficult to understand. There are some mannerly ways to treat such challenges. Experts tell us that it's the different cadence and music of a language that distracts us from the words. When our ears adjust to that difference, words become clear. You can also help yourself toward understanding by

- reducing tension. The very sound of a heavy accent can bring on nervous uncertainty about being able to understand. Relax.
- listening carefully. Focus your entire attention upon the speaker.
- being patient. Persist until your ear is able to discern the words spoken.
- listening again. Ask politely for the person to repeat what he or she said.

Language difficulty is a two-way street. Foreigners can experience tremendous confusion in hearing us speak our own language. The English spoken in America is full of things such as slang, jargon, buzz words, colloquialisms, idioms, and metaphors. So when speaking to a foreigner we should observe some rules of etiquette:

- Avoid using slang and idiomatic expressions.
- Speak clearly; don't drop consonant and vowel sounds as is often done in ordinary daily speech.
- Don't raise your voice. Volume isn't going to help you be understood.

To give you some idea why English can present such a comprehension challenge to someone from another country, consider the following from an unknown writer:

I take it you already know
Of tough and bough and cough and dough?
Others may stumble, but not you
On hiccough, thorough, slough and through.
Well don't! and now you wish, perhaps,
To learn of less familiar traps.
Beware of heard, a dreadful word
That looks like beard but sounds like bird.
And dead: it's said like bed, not bead,
For goodness sake don't call it deed!
Watch out for meat and great and threat
(They rhyme with suite and straight and debt).
A moth is not a moth as in mother
Nor both in bother, nor broth in brother,
And here is not a match for there,
Nor dear and fear for bear and pear.
And then there's dose and rose and lose—
Just look them up—and goose and choose.
And cork and work and card and ward
And font and front and word and sword
And do and go, then thwart and cart,
Come, come! I've hardly made a start.
A dreadful language? Why man alive!
I'd learned to talk it when I was five.
And yet to write it, the more I tried,
I hadn't learned it at fifty-five.

Etiquette with Disabled People

If you don't live with someone who has a disability, you may feel unsure how to behave in meeting and talking with such a person. There are a few simple principles to observe. Think in terms of what would most keep that one from feeling awkward, overly dependent, or self-conscious.

It is proper to extend your hand when meeting a disabled person. Be aware of body language, however; if he or she withdraws from physical contact, honor that preference. Don't make remarks or ask questions about the person's condition. If you have the opportunity for an extended conversation with someone in a wheelchair, sit down; it removes the awkwardness of the height differences.

Do not be condescending, and don't force unwanted help. It is proper, however, to offer assistance; the option belongs to the other person.

When you are with a person who has impaired hearing, don't shout or use exaggerated lip movements, but you may need to speak more distinctly. Be careful not to turn your face away while speaking to a person who is totally deaf.

A blind person develops other faculties that compensate for sight. Speak to him or her as you would to anyone else. If you encounter a blind person alone on a street corner, it is proper to ask if you can give assistance; don't just begin guiding or take his or her arm. If he accepts your help, let him hold your arm; it gives more confidence to be led instead of "steered" with you holding his arm. In daily situations such as entering buildings and rooms and eating, let the person indicate how much and what type of assistance is needed (for example, by describing the position of food on a plate, finding a chair, etc.). If there is a guide dog, do not play with or distract it. The animal needs to be on duty.

Visiting the Sick

Oddly, concern for folks who are sick can somehow obliterate common sense in the visitor and put strain upon the ailing one. Never make a home or hospital visit without calling ahead to get permission and a suggested time. Be genuine as you express your concern and compassion to the one who is ill, but don't gush or ask questions about treatments, diagnosis, and so forth: disclosure is at the sufferer's discretion. A verse of Scripture and brief prayer are appropriate—but not a long passage, a sermonette, or a long-winded prayer. Never stay longer than fifteen to twenty minutes; leave sooner if the person seems weary. The medical personnel and family members are in charge of the situation. If a nurse comes in, quickly excuse yourself and leave unless asked to do otherwise.

The outstanding example of self-important rudeness I've seen personally was in the hospital room of a dear friend who was battling terminal cancer. A preacher (not her own pastor) walked unannounced into the room and introduced himself at some length. The doctor entered with his nurse. The preacher looked at the medical people, said, "Let's pray," and prayed a long theological exposition. After he finally exited, and as I passed the doctor and nurse in the doorway, the expression on their faces said it all: the name of the Lord had been badly damaged.

Travel Etiquette

Travel never excuses a Christian from the requirement to be mannerly. Traveling appears to be exciting and glamorous if you don't do it. If you travel much at all, however, you find that it's exhausting and grueling. It calls upon the spirit of charity to suffer long indeed.

- Be patient. You're not the only one who's hurried, and pressured, and tired: everyone is—travelers and transportation personnel alike.
- Don't push, grumble, or be otherwise obnoxious. No one enjoys the crowds and the crush anymore than you do.
- Don't treat transportation workers like servants. Always say please and thank you. Express special commendation for those who are doing their best.
- Hold tight to a pleasant spirit. There are more than enough sour expressions and griping tongues. Make your contributions, instead, smiles and cheerful focus upon whatever positives there are.

The globe grows smaller year by year via communication advances and rapid transit. Trips to Europe and other spots around the world are no longer restricted to the rich and leisurely. International business, vacations, and mission trips have become normal.

If you have opportunity to travel abroad, there are two broad principles that should be observed. First, take particular care to represent Jesus Christ and America to the very best of your ability. Other countries are even darker spiritually than our own: they desperately need to see a lighted life walking among them. You're an ambassador of the Light of life. And represent our country well, too. The term "ugly American" didn't come into use accidentally; sadly, it has been earned. You need to counteract the phrase: in an others-focused awareness, in gracious speech, in modest, clean, and neat dress, and in a pervasive spirit of Christlikeness.

Second, know the country or countries you'll be visiting. Gather and absorb as much about each one as possible before you make the trip. It's especially important to learn ahead of time the social mores of each place so you can avoid violating them.

Feminine Charm

The word that carries the loveliest accolade for a Christian woman's attitude, actions, and appearance is "charm." Yet the meaning of that word is much befogged and distorted. In all my reading, I found the most apt definition to be the following:

Prescription for Charm

—Author Unknown

For LIPS—truth, kind words, and a smile.

For EYES—friendliness and sympathetic understanding.

For EARS—courteous attention and wholesale listening.

For HANDS—honest work and truthful deeds.

For FIGURE—helpful and right living.

For VOICE—prayer, praise, and the lilt of joy.

For HEART—love for God, for life, and for others.

I hope that as you finish reading this chapter you have had two things distinctly planted in your mind: a determination to polish your social conduct and thereby enhance your testimony and a realization that etiquette really boils down to *kindness—with style.*

Spiritual X-Rays

Take heed to yourselves, that your heart be not deceived, and ye turn aside, and serve other gods, and worship them.

You can work from now till Granny's cow comes home and your sparkly "manners" will count for nothing if you don't let them spring from and continually be oiled by the grace of God in your heart. That grace will give you eyes that see others' sensibilities and needs, a heart that reacts in compassion and concern, and a spirit that moves you to be a servant of others.

Teens

Let no man despise thy youth, but be thou an example of the believers, in word, in conversation, in charity, in spirit, in faith, in purity.

If for some reason you were able to choose only one chapter from this book for infusion into your life, I would hope it would be this one. Your attitude and behavior toward other people comprises the bulk of your public testimony. A Christ-reflecting heart of concern motivating good manners can send a beacon of eternal hope into darkened lives around you.

Mothers

That our daughters may be as corner stones, polished after the similitude of a palace.

Be encouraged by recognizing that a stone's polishing can be a long process. Sometimes in rearing a daughter we may think she'll never grasp what we want so badly to teach her. But stick with it. A polished cornerstone is not used for just any building; it's reserved for a special edifice. You have no idea where that grubby-faced tomboy may eventually serve the Lord. Don't deny her the tree-climbing, dolls-hating tendency of her early days, but aim her gently, lovingly toward greater heights and finer affections. Meanwhile, see to it that in every area of your home life you personally provide a living illustration of etiquette.

Mentors

Shewing to the generation to come the praises of the Lord, and his strength, and his wonderful works that he hath done.

As one who's slightly older and at least partially removed from the racetrack pace of earlier years, you might suggest and sponsor or host "ladyship" sessions. They could be in the form of classes or informal meetings. For instance, you could play hostess for a mother-daughter tea for which you have several mother-daughter teams prepare creative presentations of various areas requiring etiquette know-how. Or, following a series of classes on etiquette, you and your group of mothers and daughters could jointly create a formal meal at which the principles given in class are practiced.

Caution Lights

Take heed therefore that the light which is in thee be not darkness.

Out-of-kilter etiquette makes itself known in differentiation. That is, such a person determines her behavior by judging others to be worthy or unworthy of her efforts. People of position, or prominence, or power "deserve" her good manners; she hopes to impress them. But ordinary people are judged to be beneath such deserving. If that kind of thinking lurks anywhere in your mind, make a dash to the book of James, where chapter two opens with nine verses of strong, clear rebuke for Christians who operate according to such distinctions. Particularly, the fourth and ninth verses:

Are ye not then partial in yourselves, and are become judges of evil thoughts?

But if ye have respect to persons, ye commit sin, and are convinced of the law as transgressors.

CHAPTER TEN

The Ultimate Laser

CHAPTER TEN

The Ultimate Laser

For with thee is the fountain of life: in thy light shall we see light. **Ps. 36:9**

Perhaps you rationalize away any necessity for expending time and effort for self-improvement. There are several excuses commonly used to do so. But let's look at them and find out why they're not valid for a Christian woman.

As a jewel of gold in a swine's snout, so is a fair woman which is without discretion. **Prov. 11:22**

Excuse #1: "I live in a one-store town in the sand flats of Outer Podunk. There's no use in polishing myself!"

That says small-town people don't deserve your pleasing appearance and mannerly conduct. What an insult to their importance as human beings! Second, who says you will stay in Outer Podunk? Many of us started in small towns, never dreaming that we would ever live anywhere else. Only God knows where He will lead any one of His children. It is important to prepare ourselves so that our appearance, speech, and conduct are acceptable and exemplary as positive testimonies for the Lord in *any* place, within *any* stratum of society.

Excuse #2: "Oh, I *know* how to look and what to do in special situations, if I have to. But why bother on a day-to-day basis?"

That attitude actually means that you only know *about* propriety—as a passing acquaintance, so to speak. But putting on a proper image like a coat is basically dishonest, for thereby you assume a role and act a part in order to make a favorable impression at chosen times. That certainly calls your motives into question. And does Scripture ever condone dishonesty in or inconsistency of behavior?

Excuse #3: "I'm going to be a missionary; why attend to good looks and manners when I'll be living among heathen?" Because, there ought to be some distinction between you and the natives! The heathendom into which God calls missionaries is spiritual darkness. His truth-tellers are to be bearers of light—not just in word, but in life and self as well.

Excuse #4: "It's unspiritual to want to look good and to put polish on my actions!" Only if you're a cave-dwelling hermit, ma'am. Genuine spirituality translates into practical, balanced, consistent, compassionate *living*.

God does care about the appearance of that which represents Him here on earth. Think back to the earlier mention of the marvelous detail to which God gave attention when He told Moses how to build the tabernacle (Exod. 25–27) and how to clothe His priests (Exod. 28:2). The structure where He was to dwell that side of Calvary and those who served Him there utilized materials and design that were practical, valuable, and beautiful. On this side of Calvary it is we individual believers who are at once tabernacles and priests. Has God changed? Is He now grateful for and glorified by shoddy workmanship and cheap materials?

No, there really is no valid excuse against self-improvement. It is simply a matter of "whom do you love more—yourself and your ease or the Lord and others?" Believers should exhibit the *best* appearance and speech, the *most courteous* conduct of anyone on this planet—for our Christ-centered hearts prompt us to it!

Again, a new commandment I write unto you, which thing is true in him and in you: because the darkness is past, and the true light now shineth. He that saith he is in the light, and hateth his brother, is in darkness even until now. He that loveth his brother abideth in the light, and there is none occasion of stumbling in him. But he that hateth his brother is in darkness, and walketh in darkness, and knoweth not whither he goeth, because that darkness hath blinded his eyes. **I John 2:8-11**

But refuting arguments is negative; let's move on to the positive aspect of the matter and consider the principles and practicalities discussed in this book as they apply to your effectiveness as a reflector of our glorious God.

Honour and majesty are before him: strength and beauty are in his sanctuary. **Ps. 96:6**

It is of paramount importance to keep in mind, first of all, that *the scope of your social range marks the bounds of your witnessing's effectiveness.* Proper grooming, carriage, speech, and manners are acceptable on all social levels; impropriety severely limits your acceptability; and any level at which you are unacceptable means your witness is unacceptable. (There are, of course, exceptions when the Lord bypasses His normal method.) Why, as ambassadors for Christ, should we hinder our ministry through selfishness, laziness, or inverted piety? Who is going to win the "up-and-outers" with whom the Lord may bring you into contact? A standard excuse often advanced by the upper classes for rejecting "religion" is the boorishness of religion's adherents. Sadly, that objection has been given too much validity by those who nonsensically claim that "hicky is holy."

Second, *comfort contributes to communication.* Suppose you are a guest at a dinner sponsored and attended by the social leaders of your community. If you are jittery over your appearance, grammar, or table manners, your nervousness will bind your brain and tongue, making it difficult to communicate with others at the table. If, on the other hand, your refinement is natural, your freedom from tension will also be your freedom to communicate a witness for your Lord.

A third encouragement toward refining efforts is that *deference makes a difference.* The louder the world proclaims its philosophy "Do your own thing," the greater the Christian's opportunity to bear testimony through her deferential consideration for others. Self-discipline and kindness are so rare in our society that their consistent presence in a person's life draws attention and interest. That makes an effective springboard for Christian testimony.

Should you need further persuasion, go back to the epistles of Paul and note the emphasis he places upon his exemplary conduct under all circumstances. He was ever bold but never boorish. He was able to say truthfully, "I was blameless in my conduct in all things." Why did he so emphasize this aspect of his ministry? *Because his conduct gave credence to everything he wrote and spoke.* So does yours—or else it belies all you claim to believe.

Although regrettable, it is a fact that the unsaved have higher standards for Christian conduct and appearance than do many Christians themselves. Believers spend a great deal of time and energy in mental gymnastics making excuses for a life level as low as the world's. But an unregenerate person expects a "religious" individual to have superior standards in every area of life. He *wants* and *needs* to see that there is a level of living higher than his own. If the Christian flounders in the same crassness as the sinner, what inspiration, challenge, or hope can he offer? The lighted life of a believer can touch a responsive chord of yearning in the sinner's heart; the life of a mediocre Christian causes only disillusionment and contempt.

Terms and titles are cheaply purchased, or even stolen. "Christian" is indiscriminately appropriated by many individuals, institutions, and movements that actually are in opposition to Scripture principles. The only reliable way to identify that which is genuinely of Christ, therefore, is by a careful examination of motives, methods, and message in the pure light of God's Word. And, as you apply this scale of measurement to others, be aware that it simultaneously identifies you. No one can be expected to be perfect in this world—but the born-from-above believer should certainly be scripturally selfless in her motivations, scripturally separated in her methods, scripturally consistent in her life, and scripturally sound in her message. Those things will be most effectively demonstrated *in her conduct and appearance.* God does not call us women to be the theologians or preachers in His scheme of things; He *does* call us to be a *living demonstration* of His Truth.

Efforts at self-improvement should be motivated by a desire to excel *for the Lord* and must be undergirded by His own power. As in every other phase of life, you as a Christian woman have as your supplier of strength and instruction the omnipotent, omniscient, all-loving God of the universe! And within you dwells the blessed Holy Spirit, whose work (and delight) is to *refine* us by His pure fire.

When you lay aside this book, I pray that you will pick up a burden to let God's Word constantly be used of the Holy Spirit to illuminate your heart and mind and to extend that light more clearly into every aspect of your appearance, speech, and conduct. We live in a darkening world. However, by God's grace we walk a different pathway:

> But the path of the just is as the shining light, that shineth more and more unto the perfect day. **Prov. 4:18**

It is for the sake of your testimony as a thoroughly lovely Christian lady that this book has been written. May you lift your eyes from these pages to the blessed face of your Savior, whose matchless, beautiful light we are to reflect. In, through, and for Him each one of us can and should live **in the best possible light.**